THE WRITER'S GUIDE TO
COPYRIGHT, CONTRACT AND LAW

Visit our How To website at www.howto.co.uk

At **www.howto.co.uk** you can engage in conversation with our authors - all of whom have 'been there and done that' in their specialist fields. You can get access to special offers and additional content but most importantly you will be able to engage with, and become a part of, a wide and growing community of people just like yourself.

At **www.howto.co.uk** you'll be able to talk and share tips with people who have similar interests and are facing similar challenges in their lives. People who, just like you, have the desire to change their lives for the better – be it through moving to a new country, starting a new business, growing their own vegetables, or writing a novel.

At **www.howto.co.uk** you'll find the support and encouragement you need to help make your aspirations a reality.

Visit **www.writers-guide-to-copyright-contract-and-law.co.uk**

How To Books strives to present authentic, inspiring, practical information in their books. Now, when you buy a title from **How To Books,** you get even more than just words on a page.

4TH EDITION

THE WRITER'S GUIDE TO COPYRIGHT, CONTRACT AND LAW

HOW TO ENJOY YOUR RIGHTS AS AN AUTHOR AND COMPLY WITH YOUR OBLIGATIONS

HELEN SHAY

howtobooks

Published by How To Books Ltd,
Spring Hill House, Spring Hill Road,
Begbroke, Oxford OX5 1RX. United Kingdom.
Tel: (01865) 375794. Fax: (01865) 379162.
info@howtobooks.co.uk
www.howtobooks.co.uk

How To Books greatly reduce the carbon footprint of their books by sourcing their typesetting
and printing in the UK.

First edition 1996
Second edition 2000
Third edition 2005
Fourth edition 2009

British Library Cataloguing in Publication Data
A catalogue record for this book is available from the British Library

ISBN 978 1 84528 321 6

Produced for How To Books by Deer Park Productions, Tavistock, Devon
Typeset by PDQ Typesetting, Newcastle-under-Lyme, Staffs.
Printed and bound by Bell & Bain Ltd, Glasgow

NOTE: The material contained in this book is set out in good faith for general guidance and
no liability can be accepted for loss or expense incurred as a result of relying in particular
circumstances on statements made in the book. The laws and regulations are complex and
liable to change, so readers should check the current position with the relevant authorities and
take advice on specific circumstances before making personal arrangements.

Contents

List of Illustrations

Foreword

In a long career as a writer I've seen hard times come and then go. But the present hard times may be, like King Charles, an unconscionable time a-dying.

After abandonment of the Net Book Agreement, publishers were murmuring they wanted to renegotiate contracts; newspaper chains have been trying to grab all the electronic rights in articles submitted to them; magazines seem less willing to take freelance work and if they do, delay payment; TV production companies impose very severe rules about looking at a new author's work; and a new, and cleverer, race of vanity publishers seems ready to trick an inexperienced poet or book author.

Our writing world is changing very fast and not, it seems, to our advantage. It is vital not to let ourselves be exploited or diminished in face of new technology and new circumstances. We may find we need to assert ourselves, to insist on our rights.

You ask: What are my rights? Simply *knowing a few facts* is often enough to reduce a troublesome editor or publisher to order.

With this book, you have in Helen Shay a source of help at hand at all times – from someone who cares about writers!

Jean Bowden
Past Chairman of the Society of Women Writers and Journalists,
Past Chairman of the Crime Writers Association.
As Tessa Barclay, author of many novels
published by Headline Books

Preface to the Fourth Edition

When I wrote the first edition of this book over 12 years ago, I could not imagine the dramatic changes that would subsequently take place in publishing and the writing environment. Perhaps I should have done. After all, don't we as writers know more than most that truth often proves stranger than fiction? This is especially so in our own area, due to new technology and Internet growth. Whilst hopefully this will not spell the end of the book as we know it, new developments like ebooks and reader devices have made electronic rights of paramount importance, whilst more traditional legal areas still impact upon us. The law has more significance than ever in a writer's life.

In just the three years since the third edition, the legal field has changed rapidly, bringing both new protection and new challenges for writers. This edition updates and enlarges upon previous material, and also places additional emphasis on contract. This is reflected in the new title, amended to *The Writer's Guide to Copyright, Contract and Law*. There are now three chapters on contract, including one focusing on Negotiating a Publishing Contract. This is because contractual matters have increasing importance in the career of a successful writer. Similarly, the case studies used have been added to and altered where necessary, to be more relevant to current topical situations.

After a decade that has seen wide-ranging legislative activity, we have perhaps reached a point where we can now take stock. European law has had a major influence, sometimes bringing helpful new rights to assist writers. Changes to data protection regulation have been implemented (though recent controversy over lost data may herald other changes to come). Reform of civil court procedure has been put in place and has had special impact on libel actions. Court cases, such as that involving *The Da Vinci Code*, have reinforced existing copyright law, whereas others (one currently involving the renowned children's author, J. K. Rowling) may help illuminate developing legal areas. Further caselaw has clarified matters, such as the '*Reynolds* defence' against libel claims, which can now benefit authors as well as journalists. More changes are also unfolding following the recent government-commissioned *Gowers Review* on intellectual property. Challenges for writers continue with the growth of print on demand (POD) technology and the current practice of heavy discounting by some publishers.

Against this background, the book essentially sets out to provide a basic and accessible guide to the legal context of writing, as regards the law of England and Wales. Hopefully, the book as significantly updated and augmented remains a helpful guide and continues to meet a need, as when it first appeared in 1996. Over the years, I personally have gained much fulfillment in writing and revising it, including working with the publisher and meeting other writers through it, such as when guest speaking at writing events. It is primarily aimed at less experienced writers, providing an overview of the provisions that can affect them. Whilst not intended as a substitute for professional advice on specific situations, it sets out to steer them in the right direction. (Where changes have not been fully implemented or have only been recently introduced, I have tried to predict possible implications, but readers should check the current position from time to time.)

I would like to thank those who have assisted with relevant information and friends and colleagues (both in legal and writing spheres), who have passed on their own experiences to contribute to case studies. I am also grateful for the help of my editor, Nikki Reed, and to the supportive writers' organisations of which I am privileged to be a member, in particular The Society of Authors and the Society of Women Writers and Journalists.

Finally, even though as writers we now work within a more complex writing world, let us not overlook the new opportunities that have also arisen, such as online markets or self-publishing (where costs have tumbled and many writers have found this an empowering way to be successful). At the time of writing, the National Year for Reading is underway and there is renewed enthusiasm to celebrate the written word. So get writing – and using (not losing) your copyright!

Helen Shay

(Postscript – It is perhaps a sign of the present unusual times that there has been a little longer period than normal between writing and publication of this edition. Writers, along with publishers and other sectors, have been affected by the economic uncertainties, and now need more than ever to guard their rights. However, the need for good literature has probably never been greater, with all the non-materialistic enrichment it can bring to readers.)

What Use Are Your Rights?

If a man knows the law, there is nothing he cannot do when he likes.
(*Vera*, Oscar Wilde)

HOW IMPORTANT IS THE LAW TO YOU AS A WRITER?

This book aims to help you, the writer, to:

- enjoy your full rights;

- avoid legal pitfalls;

- eliminate any come-back upon you.

It may be particularly useful to 'up and coming' writers. They cannot yet command 'the clout' of the bestsellers and established writers, so often find that their lack of bargaining power is a threat to a fulfilling career.

Writing and the law have much in common. Words are their mutual stock-in-trade. Both aim to use these to a precise effect: the one to engage the reader; the other to define (or even bend) the rules within which society operates. Because of this, you as a writer are especially equipped to understand the subtleties of the law. And it is best that you should. It affects your working life, whether you recognise it or not:

- during the writing process itself;

- in approaches and negotiations for publication;

- on publication and thereafter.

The law is of great significance to you as a writer. Knowledge of it is power.

Main areas of law helpful to a writer

Copyright: which gives you the author control over your work. It cannot be copied, published, produced or adapted without your agreement.

Moral rights: which are attached to copyright and give you the right to be identified as author of the work and to object to any derogatory treatment of it.

Rights entitlement: so that you as copyright owner can grant licences for dealings with the work – and on agreed financial terms.

Contract law: which can aid you in informal and formal dealings with publishers attempting to 'call the shots'. Getting the right terms can significantly improve the benefit you obtain from your work.

Law of confidence: which can protect the material you discuss with a third party.

Debt-collecting procedures: to help you to obtain due payment with minimum fuss and expense.

Wills and trusts: which can safeguard your wishes as regards what happens to your work in the future.

(Note – the law in the context of this book is generally that of England and Wales as it applies to UK citizens.)

IS THE LAW AN ASS?

For you as a writer, the law can offer constant protection. For example, it usually recognises the existence of your copyright – without which your work could be stolen, copied and/or misused – as the words flow from your pen or are recorded on PC. The law is also there to help construe a contract in any commercial dealings with your work – sometimes even where this is not embodied in a signed document. If you are not paid under such a contract, then redress does exist for you. Therefore, ass or not, the law can be of use to you.

However, there is some rough with the smooth. Certain legal sanctions can be very dangerous for writers. The law of libel can trap even the innocent, if careless. A writer may also unknowingly transgress the boundaries of plagiarism. The financial penalty and damage to literary reputation can be disastrous. You need to know when to exercise caution.

WATCHING OUT FOR LEGAL DANGERS

A writer is more at risk from proceedings in that the evidence is usually there – written down for all to see. For example, an action for slander (basically, spoken abuse, as opposed to libel which is the written form) may often fail for lack of proof. A writer, however, cannot deny what he or she said in print.

Main legal danger zones for a writer
- Infringing someone else's copyright, through direct or indirect copying. Although general ideas themselves have no copyright, if you write something too similar to another's work, whether unintentionally or not and despite however cleverly paraphrased, there can be problems.

- Quoting too much from another's material or drawing upon specialised research without permission or acknowledgement.

- Libelling someone whether by express reference, by implication or disguised as a fictional character.

- Entering a contract without appreciating onerous terms within it – or even that it is a contract.

- Failing to make adequate provision in your will for what happens to your work, so that your literary affairs become mismanaged and the future of your work suffers.

GAINING THE REWARDS OF KNOWING YOUR RIGHTS

The law is present in your writing career. You can use it, break it or ignore it. The last two are at your peril. The first can mean:

- The fruits of your labours remain your own – not a springboard for others to manipulate.

- You enter contracts with your eyes open, ready to object and negotiate over any unreasonable terms.

- You do not enter contracts by accident through informal correspondence.

- You receive increased income from safeguarded royalties and licensing arrangements.

- You can take action to secure prompt payment, including proceedings if necessary.

- You can meet force with force in any dispute and, from as strong a position as possible, reach a good settlement.

CASE STUDIES – INTRODUCTION

The fictional case studies below introduce three writers whose imaginary situations we will follow in the succeeding chapters. Each works within a different literary field. The law will be the same for each, but because of their particular aims, the implications may affect them in different ways.

Although there is never a 'typical' writer, as we are all individual, the characters and situations here are based on research undertaken with writing groups/organisations and feedback given by creative writing tutors, plus legal advisers working in this field.

Whilst neither the case studies nor any other information in this book can cover specific circumstances which may arise in any individual case (and neither are intended as a substitute for professional advice), they may give you useful pointers relevant to common situations.

Liz Burnett, novelist, short story and article writer

Liz is a fiction writer in her early thirties. She has managed to combine domestic commitments with a promising writing career. She began with stories for popular women's magazines (for which market she still writes occasionally) but now concentrates on novels. She also writes the odd article, usually commissioned through her magazine contacts.

Bill Sellars, poet and biographer

Bill is a former history teacher, in his sixties. His retirement has given him the opportunity to develop his talent for poetry, with work accepted by some literary publications. He is also producing a biography from research into a local Victorian social reformer.

Daniel Charleton, playwright and screen-writer

Daniel is a dramatist in his mid-forties. Although he 'dabbled in writing' from an early age, most of his working life was spent in the army, which he left several years ago because of ill-health. He was always unsettled in his 'civvy-street' job. When made redundant, he decided to concentrate on writing. He attended a residential course with a well-respected organisation and found his forte in drama. His plays have been produced by amateur groups, with one taken to the Fringe. Some of his comedy material has been used in radio shows. He is currently working on a sit-com, having received a positive response to his proposal from an independent TV production company.

SUMMARY

Essential law for writers:

◆ copyright;

◆ libel;

◆ contract;

◆ litigation;

◆ wills/trusts.

POINTS TO CONSIDER

1. Consider whether you have to apply for copyright in your work.

2. Defamation is the collective legal term for libel and slander. Which of these will affect you most as a writer?

3. What kind of dealings with a publisher could potentially amount to a binding contract?

Using Your Copyright

...to protect, in as effective and uniform a manner as possible, the rights of authors in their literary and artistic works

(Underlying desire stated in the Berne Convention, as revised)

WHAT IS COPYRIGHT?

Basically it is the right to allow (or not to allow) anyone to copy your work. Under our law, it can arise **automatically** through the mere act of writing. Every original literary work you create is vested magically as it appears in a tangible form with the legal by-product of copyright.

For instance, the above paragraph is now copyright. Similarly neither this book nor any substantial part of it can be reproduced without permission. (There are limited exceptions – see Chapter 3.)

'How can I apply for copyright for my book?' is a common question from novice writers. The answer is 'You don't' (as hopefully you replied to the first Points to Consider in Chapter 1). The confusion often arises because you must apply for a patent for inventions and to register a trade mark. The same formalities do not generally attach to owning copyright in this country.

◆ Where you produce work **in the course of employment**, copyright usually belongs to your employer, unless there is a contract stating otherwise.

Copyright is in what you write – not what you think
It is very difficult to gain legal protection over mere ideas.

This has recently been emphasised in the much-publicised legal case involving Dan Brown's best-selling novel *The Da Vinci Code*. It was asserted that this made unauthorised use of themes and materials in the non-fiction work *The Holy Blood and the Holy Grail* by Michael Baigent, Richard Leigh and Henry Lincoln. The court did not agree that there had been copyright infringement and the challengers had to pay hefty legal fees. It is the expression of the idea, rather than the idea itself that is protected.

Example
Suppose you discuss the ingenious plot of your next thriller at a writers' seminar. Sometime later you find that the quiet one in the corner has announced that a publisher has accepted his novel based on a similar story. This type of situation can rarely give rise to a legal claim.

Always get it down in writing. Then you will gain copyright as regards your own written format and anything very similar can be challenged.

The court in *The Da Vinci Code* case offered a checklist of points to assess the strength of a claim on the following lines:

- What are the similarities between the two works?
- What access did the alleged infringer have to your work?
- Did the alleged infringer actually make some use of your work?
- If he/she denies this, what explanation can they give for similarities?

◆ If use was made, did this amount to 'a substantial part'? (See Chapter 3.)

What sort of right is copyright?

As it affects writers, it is mainly 'civil'. This does not mean a civil right like freedom of speech. Here it signifies that you can enforce your rights as an individual through the civil court system (see Chapter 8).

Most rights relevant to writers are civil, as you will see as you progress through this book. In some instances the criminal law steps in, including criminal offences relating to copyright. The police usually only become involved where there is modern-day 'piracy' – for example, unauthorised editions or large-scale pirated copies of books. Sometimes Trading Standard Departments (you should find the address of your local one in *Yellow Pages*) will implement such prosecutions in the magistrates' courts. Private prosecutions *can* be taken out, though some people have taken this step and found it can back-fire, proving embarrassing and costly.

Unauthorised downloading of material via the Internet has become of increasing concern in recent years. It has, for example, been estimated that some £500,000 of illegal audio versions of *Harry Potter* may have been distributed. A 2005 government-funded study highlighted that consumers simply do not appreciate that unauthorised downloading can equate to shoplifting; rather it is seen as acceptable. Struggling writers take a different view. Measures against this include efforts by the Society of Authors, the Publishers Association and the Alliance against IP Theft. The Writers' Guild strike in America in early 2008 was settled with recognition of entitlement to a fair share of benefit from new media and the Internet market. In the UK, a recent government report has led to increased powers for Trading Standards Officers applying where there is copyright infringement without necessarily also involving trademark infringement.

What are the legal remedies?

The orders which the civil courts can make include:

+ An injunction – to stop publication of infringing work.

+ Damages – to compensate you. (Additional damages can be awarded for flagrant infringement.)

+ An account of profits – so that you take over the profits made by an infringing act. (This is an alternative to damages.)

+ An order for 'delivery up' /seizure/destruction of items containing the infringement. (This can be expensive for publishers, so threat of it can encourage a favourable settlement.)

You may find that any challenge you make is settled before proceedings have to be commenced (see also Chapter 8). Involving a solicitor will probably add authority to your challenge and 'encourage' a favourable settlement.

Damages have been usually based on notional royalties, but a recent government report recommends possibly increasing these, as a deterrent against infringement.

How long does copyright last?

Under UK law, the period for a long time was basically for the author's life plus a further 50 years. A European Directive extended the 50 to 70 years, calculated from the end of the calendar year of the author's death. This was intended to harmonise the position throughout Europe. It was implemented here by Parliament through The Duration of Copyright and Rights in Performances Regulations 1995. This has given rise to various complications, particularly regarding 'revived' and 'extended' copyright in some works.

What is copyright worth?

That depends on the saleability of your manuscript. Nevertheless, there may be potential value, even in what you consider to be your minor pieces. If you manage to publish several novels, you may find the short stories which you used for 'teething' are attractive to a publisher for an anthology.

◆ **Resist** any attempt by a publisher to obtain full copyright and control over your works (see Chapter 5).

How do you prove copyright?

If the work is published in the UK, there is little problem in establishing legal protection. But how do you prove that you wrote an unpublished work before anyone else?

Some organisations offer a service of registering unpublished works on a database for a fee. Recently these have been administered particularly via websites offering to 'register authors' copyrights'. This might be seen as an excessive precaution to have to take. If you could only prove your right through such measures it would go against the spirit of the Berne Convention (discussed later). This stresses that no formal procedure should be necessary to gain copyright.

In any dispute, however, the courts might find it difficult to grant you an order, if simply faced with 'one word against another'. In civil cases, the onus of proof is upon the individual making a claim to prove his allegations on a balance of probabilities. You must bring some evidence to sway the balance. Items such as diary notes have been used in court. Witnesses may be available; for example, someone to whom you showed your manuscript for critical comment. Don't forget that your own testimony is still some evidence, though obviously the self-interest factor makes it carry less weight. PC evidence, such as a hard disc showing dates involved, can help.

For important work over which you are very concerned, a precaution can be to post a sealed copy to yourself and retain this unopened with its dated postmark. (It is also there as a back-up hard copy in real emergencies. Jilly Cooper once told how she left the only copy of a manuscript on a bus and had to rewrite the lot – though it still became a bestseller.)

What about copyright notices?

The familiar © symbol is prescribed by the Universal Copyright Convention (see later) and is a necessary part of claiming copyright in some countries. Whilst not a legal necessity to claim copyright here, it is still useful to include on your material as a 'warning shot' that you will actively guard your copyright. It can also help you defeat a defence of **innocent infringement** (such as when someone maintains that they genuinely did not know that copyright subsisted in the work) and thus allow you to recover damages.

You can simply insert

© 20XX (*your name*)

or go further by also adding a clause similar to Figure 1. (As regards the 1988 legislation mentioned, you will study this later in this chapter.)

Fig. 1. Copyright notice.

What are the origins of copyright?

Parliament has recognised this right since the eighteenth century. Until recently it has been treated in this country as primarily a type of property right. It is perhaps significant of our mercantile past that UK law has, in one sense, seen creativity as a commodity. Copyright is referred to technically as a type of **intellectual property**. Other European states arguably had a more altruistic recognition of the creator's right, such as in France through *droits de suite* (resale royalty rights) and *droits moraux* (moral rights) which have existed there for some time.

The international background has come to influence our law, particularly through **conventions** (types of charter) signed by several countries. The four main copyright conventions are:

◆ Berne;
◆ Universal Copyright;
◆ Rome;
◆ Geneva.

Only the first two really affect literary copyright. Of those, Berne gives greater protection to authors and now covers most major countries.

The idea behind these conventions is that the countries who sign up to them will regulate the rights of authors in similar ways.

New technology has created a need to revise conventions to reflect developments, this work being mainly undertaken through the **World Intellectual Property Organisation (WIPO)**, linked to the United Nations and based in Geneva. The Internet and developments like MP3 files, P2P networks and podcasting have created particular challenges with which the law has struggled to keep up and protect rights, particularly in the field of music.

The Act

The influence of conventions was partly behind the introduction of the **Copyright, Designs and Patents Act 1988**. If you remember only one technical legal authority, make it this one. It is 'the Act' and is referred to as such in the rest of this chapter. Your rights under it are the cards in your hand when you negotiate any deal with a publisher.

Figure 2 lists the main rights together with the section of the Act in which each appears. (The Act has been amended and up-dated, in particular as a result of EU directives.)

KNOWING YOUR 'MORAL RIGHTS'

What are your moral rights?

Every law student learns – if they did not know already – that law

RIGHTS	SECTION
Copyright – the 'property right' which exists in every original literary, dramatic, musical or artistic work.	1
The exclusive right to copy the work and issue copies of it to the public.	2, 17 and 18
The exclusive right to perform, show or play the work in public.	2 and 19
The exclusive right to broadcast the work or include it in a cable programme service.	2 and 20
The exclusive right to make an adaptation of the work.	2 and 21
The right (a) to assign (i.e. sell/give) the whole copyright or just some rights (as mentioned above) attached to it, provided it is done in writing and signed by you; (b) to give a licence to allow the work to be published or dealt with in a particular way; (c) to leave your copyright to a specified person in your will.	90
The right to assign/license copyright in future works.	91
Moral rights.	77 – 89

Fig. 2. Table of rights in the Copyright, Designs and Patents Act 1988.

and morality are rarely the same. The one can, however, influence the other. For example, Victorian morality upheld the law which sent Oscar Wilde to prison for homosexuality and which later more liberal attitudes helped abolish. As regards copyright, 'moral rights' is a technical term for **legal provisions aimed at preserving an author's literary reputation**.

At one time, the only moral rights which the English courts recognised in this area seem to have been their own. They would not enforce copyright protection for a work which they regarded as immoral. Just after the First World War, a novel was viewed by a judge as portraying adultery too attractively. The author was denied legal redress for breach of copyright. Such attitudes took effect more as arbitrary censorship (later blasted away by the 1960s trial concerning D.H. Lawrence's novel *Lady Chatterley's Lover*). They did not give much recognition to the status of the writer.

The Act brought in express moral rights. These are:

- **The right to be identified as the author** when the work is published, performed, broadcast, included in a film or sound recording, or adapted.

- **The right to object to derogatory treatment of work** through something being inserted or deleted, or any other alteration or adaptation made when it is published, performed, broadcast or included in a cable programme, film or sound recording.

- **The right not to be falsely attributed as author of work**, so that such work cannot wrongly benefit from your name and standing.

Why are these important?

Paternity right
This is the name for the first moral right listed above (perhaps sexist, but accepted terminology). It is essential to get credit for your work at every opportunity. An example is, of course, when sales in a novel increase following dramatisation on television. The author needs to be properly credited, especially if the adaptation has a different title from the original. (For example, Stephen King's short story, *The Body*, which was not in his most characteristic style, formed the basis for the successful film, *Stand By Me*.)

Integrity right
This is the second moral right. Whilst it may not have the same economic worth as the paternity right, it matters a great deal to writers. There are easier ways of making money, and the writer is usually also motivated by the need to communicate a particular idea in a particular way. To see that distorted can be devastating. It is said that Anthony Burgess was mortified at the film adaptation of *A Clockwork Orange*. (This was pre-Act.) There have also been Hollywood battles involving committed directors, such as Terry Gilliam, who wished his – rather than Universal Studios' – version of *Brazil* to be released. Artistic and commercial interests often clash. Changes detrimental to a work can injure the creator's credibility and career.

Objections
You cannot object to every change made to your work (otherwise editors would be out of a job). Treatment is only 'derogatory' if it **distorts or mutilates your work or prejudices your 'honour or reputation'**. The case law is limited, but what seems to be involved

is something which changes the artistic impact. For example, a director cut a specific stage direction for a West End production of Samuel Beckett's *Footfalls*. The direction indicated that a character should walk several paces forward and back during the play. The estate of the playwright (acting through his agent) objected and successfully insisted that this be put back in. Given the title and the author's reputation (even aside from any licence conditions), there must be a strong argument that a stage direction of this sort was vital to the integrity of the work.

Exceptions

There are several exceptions. Important ones to note include:

♦ There is no paternity or integrity right over work for publication in a newspaper, magazine, periodical, encyclopaedia, or other such collective work or for news broadcasts. This is therefore relevant to many freelance writers and could affect academics writing for journals.

♦ The integrity right does not apply to translations.

False attribution

The third moral right protects you against false attribution. It will mainly apply when you are rich and famous, and someone falsely insinuates that you are the author of work, in order to trade on your reputation. (This right previously existed under older 1956 legislation.) It can sometimes be used for such as newspaper dramatised accounts that purport to be by someone involved.

PRESERVING THESE RIGHTS

You must **assert in writing your right to be identified as author**. This could be by a small print notice on your work such as:

The right of (*insert your name*) to be identified as author of this work, pursuant to s 77 of the Copyright, Designs and Patents Act 1988, is hereby asserted.

You can assert the right in relation to a pen name – but you must specify this.

It is important not to accidentally forgo moral rights, such as through implication in correspondence. This might, for example, arise if a publisher wrote to you offering a fee for 'full rights' and you accepted without clarifying this phrase. This is because, in law, something known as an 'estoppel' can arise to prevent you going back on something agreed, whatever your true intention at the time. Another example might be if a publisher sent you a form including a waiver (letting-go) of your rights, which you returned unsigned but without expressly rejecting it, and meanwhile agreed to publication over the telephone.

On a more general level, it is worth noting that the recent launch by the Federation of Screenwriters in Europe of the **European Screenwriters' Manifesto** has been backed by over 20 national writers' guilds, reinforcing the need to honour moral rights and calling for better overall treatment. Another initiative emphasising moral rights is 'Texts Don't Grow on Trees', launched by the **European Writers' Congress**. As regards copyright in general, a recent Green Paper calls for Internet service providers to take responsibility for policing how customers use the Internet. This may herald changes to curb infringement and piracy. It echoes calls from the music industry, such as in the strong protest made by the manager of U2 rock group.

NOTING OTHER RIGHTS

You have looked at the core rights given by the Act, but there are others. A statutory instrument gave authors and performers who have transferred their rental right for a sound recording or film to a producer, the **right to receive equitable remuneration** for the rental of their works after 1 April 1997. This law applied automatically to works made under agreements dated after 1 July 1994. (For those dated earlier, you had to give notice before 1997.) Often rights such as this can be administered through **collecting societies**, such as the **Authors' Licensing and Collecting Society (ALCS)**, if you obtain membership (free to members of the **National Union of Journalists**, the **Society of Authors** and/or **Writers' Guild of Great Britain**).

Other examples now include special rights for databases (see Chapter 3). There have also been significant developments regarding 'electronic rights' (see Chapter 5).

AVOIDING INFRINGEMENT OF COPYRIGHT

Whilst the law protects your work, there is a corresponding obligation upon you not to infringe the rights of others. If you wish to use or draw upon another's work, pay heed to the following guidelines:

- First consider whether the work is still copyright or in 'the public domain' (i.e. has copyright expired?). This is obvious with, for example, Shakespeare, but be especially careful with more recent writers from the late nineteenth century onwards. The introduction of the 70-year period brought with it complicated transitional provisions, including some for 'revived' and 'extended' copyrights.

◆ Note also, that a publisher can sometimes claim copyright in a typographical arrangement. This copyright basically lasts for **25 years**.

◆ If the work is in copyright, then copying it is restricted (see Chapter 3).

◆ If you infringe copyright by accident, when you did not know and had no reason to believe there was copyright in the work, you may have the defence of innocent infringement. Usually you are not ordered to pay compensation (though publication of your infringing work will normally be stopped).

Warning
There is a copyright equivalent of an urban myth often repeated that as long as you change seven things, there will never be any infringement. This is nonsense and has no legal foundation.

CASE STUDIES

Liz is 'robbed'
Liz naturally had several short story rejections in addition to her acceptances. She is shocked to find that a 'twist in the tail' story which she failed to place has appeared in a magazine under someone else's name.

Liz's records show that this story was rejected two years ago by a magazine based in the same building and being part of the same company group, as the one publishing the story. She suspects the editor who returned it as unsuitable, of giving a copy to a colleague in another division. Then she notices something familiar about the name under which the story appears. She recalls it was a pen name used by a member of a writers' group she formerly attended. She and the member had swapped work for mutual criticism, until this person shunned her after Liz began to have some success.

The editor proves to be a red herring. (Whilst many editors work under tight budgets and are not necessarily saint-like individuals, most are professionals who would not risk their reputation through such shoddy behaviour.) The real villain is the jealous ex-friend, who is finding it difficult to get anywhere by her own efforts. Liz has the evidential burden of showing that she wrote the story. A rejection may prove of use for once. The editor is unlikely to remember or wish to become involved, but the rejecting letter may provide corroboration. Liz may possibly also have the statement of another third party to whom she showed the story, together with her original drafts and computer data.

Her most effective course is to approach the magazine publishing the story. It will probably be anxious to avoid litigation/bad press and promote a settlement. Liz should hold out for a reasonable amount as regards the lost fee and opportunity for publication under her name. It may be possible to negotiate that the magazine print one of her other stories at a future date.

Bill wants to 'borrow'
In the biography of his eminent Victorian, Bill wants to quote several long passages from the diary of a nineteenth-century contemporary.

Bill needs to establish whether the diary is still in copyright. As a starting point, he will have to check the year of death of the diarist and add on seventy years from the end of that year.

Bill may have a problem because the copyright could still be in existence and possibly 'revived' by the legal changes. The provisions are very complicated, so he must be careful. Other relevant factors here may be whether the diary was published or not, and whether published posthumously, as this can, in some circumstances, affect the duration of copyright. To be on the safe side, Bill may have to approach the diarist's descendants or publisher (if any) to ascertain who is the present copyright owner, and obtain permission, probably incurring a fee. If he decides instead simply to mention the fact of the association of his subject with the diarist, then he need not take these steps.

In the search for a copyright holder, **ALCS** or CLA may sometimes be able to help (address at the back of this book). In recent years, there has also been a project called **WATCH (Writers Artists and their Copyright Holders)**. It compiled a list of many copyright holders organised by author's surname.

A recent government report has also pressed for changes in the law to make it easier to reproduce 'orphan works' (where the author cannot be traced after reasonable attempts). This will especially help historians and biographers like Bill.

Daniel is adaptable

One of Daniel's plays is staged by a small company and receives favourable local press coverage. A radio station approaches him to adapt and broadcast this. At first he is flattered and gives his consent. This particular play, however, is a little more than his usual comedy pieces. It includes some political satire which the station intends to cut. He is therefore having second thoughts.

Daniel should argue over this on the basis of his integrity right. Treatment is, however, only derogatory if it amounts to a distortion or mutilation of the play or damages Daniel's 'honour or reputation'. He could try to contest that to remove the serious element will damage his reputation if the work now appears merely flippant.

The best solution is probably for Daniel to discuss the matter with the station. As he wants the broadcast to go ahead, Daniel should avoid being adversarial. He could aim for a compromise, whereby some of the producer's reservations are taken into account but with as few cuts to the text as possible.

A writer like Daniel also needs to be careful about input received from others in developing a script especially if, for example, the director is making additions as well as cuts. In one case, a director wrote an opening scene, introducing characters and plot elements. The author later used this in a successful production of the work. The court found an 'implied licence' for the author to do so, but in the future, a direct licence from the director would have to be obtained.

SUMMARY

- Under our law, you usually obtain copyright automatically in what you write. Always get it down on paper/PC/beermat – whatever you choose – as soon as you can.

- Whilst not a UK legal requirement, putting a copyright notice on your work, such as the familiar © followed by name and year can 'warn-off' would-be copiers and help defeat any defence of innocent infringement.

- If very concerned that your unpublished work could be copied, post a sealed copy to yourself so that it bears the date of posting (or leave it with, for example, a bank or solicitor, obtaining their dated receipt) to provide evidence of when it was written by you.

- The Copyright, Designs and Patents Act 1988 gives you rights which are your bargaining tools in negotiating any contract.

- Your paternity right has to be asserted in writing. Include this in any contract with a publisher (see also Chapter 5).

- Beware informal arrangements which imply that you forgo any of your 'moral rights'.

- If you wish to draw upon another writer's material, check whether it is in copyright. If it is, follow the guidelines given in Chapter 3.

POINTS TO CONSIDER

1. If you were in a similar position to Liz in the case study, what sort of evidence could you bring to support your case? Consider how you deal with your work, with a view to keeping simple records of its development, copies and details of submissions with dates.

2. Devise a simple copyright notice in small font, consisting of at least ©, your name and the year, to position discreetly on your work.

3. What sort of unauthorised changes to your work (beyond normal editing) would you regard as infringing your integrity right?

3

Utilising Material

... laws were like cobwebs; where the small flies were caught, and the great break through.

(*Apothegms*, Francis Bacon)

INPUTTING SOURCES WITHIN YOUR TEXT

By and large, facts, news, general ideas and information do not have copyright. On the face of it, therefore, you have a free hand when it comes to the sources you wish to build upon in your work.

That said, you must be careful if you are basing your work, or part of it, on lines similar to those of another which is in copyright. If you are a non-fiction writer, for example, you must go back to the original authorities rather than rely on any existing book which you are trying to better/rival. Mere paraphrasing, however careful, is always dangerous and unethical.

Selection

This also applies as regards the selection of material. For example, if you wanted to write a book of questions and answers on technical matters, you cannot take the framework used in a similar work. You must structure your own questions and answers from scratch.

Presentation

The presentation of factual information has often been protected by copyright. One judge said this depended upon 'the requisite degree of skill, judgement and labour' which had gone into selection and presentation. The law covering databases has also made the situation more complex.

Rights for databases

Under the legislation, many things can potentially amount to a database, such as a mailing list or a list of source material, research data and collections of material accessible online or on CD-Rom, for example a multimedia encyclopaedia. In basic terms, in order to qualify material has to be arranged in a systematic or methodical way, and be accessible by electronic *or* other means. Such work could then have copyright protection if, due to the selection or arrangement of the contents, the database **constitutes the author's own intellectual creation**.

There is also a special **database right** for databases made on or after 1 January 1983 by someone who is a national of or habitually resident in the EEA. This right lasts (in general terms) for 15 years – but is repeatable if material is significantly updated during that period. It can exist even when the database does not have copyright protection, provided there has been 'substantial investment in obtaining, verifying or presenting the contents'. The 'investment' can be financial, human or technical.

Basically, this means you cannot make use (the legislation refers to 'extraction or re-utilisation') of the database without getting permission. Even small parts could amount to infringement, particularly if you keep using them. 'Fair dealing' for research or private study (see later in this chapter) applies to databases, but *not* if you are doing this for a commercial purpose. You must generally indicate the source of the data.

The limited caselaw in this area has indicated that protection for databases may not be so wide. If you own a database and wish to claim/preserve rights in it, it can help if you:

♦ update this regularly so that the 15-year protection period may recommence;

♦ place a copyright notice on this with your name, year and statement that 'All rights are reserved, including database right';

♦ keep a record of the time and effort put into the database and invested in the organisation and arrangement of it.

Be aware that Data Protection provisions will often apply to databases (see later in this chapter).

Letters

This area sometimes causes confusion. Note that copyright applies to letters as to other writing. The recipient owns the actual letter, but the writer owns copyright in the contents (unless agreed otherwise).

Special rules can apply to unpublished letters available for public inspection, for example in a museum or library. These depend on the age of the letters and the time which has elapsed since the death of the writer.

Acknowledgement

It is safest and professional courtesy to acknowledge sources. It is a good idea to learn how to use the footnote or endnote functions in software programs such as Word. This will help you cite sources and build up a bibliography (including authors' names, book titles, publishers and dates of publication). Also reference any source found on the Internet.

This is not really required where information is **common knowledge**. Sometimes it is difficult to be sure if this is the case, or whether only the skill and labour of another author made the data available. If in doubt, acknowledge (see later).

HOW MUCH CAN YOU QUOTE?

A matter of some substance
You can be guilty of an infringement if you use without permission any **substantial part** of a work in copyright.

The courts look at the circumstances in each case. Even a tiny part can be enough if it is the crux of the original work. A film company infringed copyright by using 20 seconds of a four-minute tune without permission. In another case, however, the use of four lines of a song as chapter headings was allowed (but it is advisable always to obtain permission to quote song lyrics in copyright). It is neither quality nor quantity that matters, but what the courts see as **substantiality**.

In a recent case involving Prince Charles's private journals, the court found against a newspaper that used comments from these without permission. Although only relatively small parts were taken, these were the attention-drawing parts. (Breach of confidentiality was also relevant here.)

A few short words
Fortunately writers are helped by the **de minimus rule**. (This is the

first lawyer's Latin encountered in this book. You will get used to it.) It means that the courts will not interfere with the use of small and trivial pieces of another's work.

Basically this has the effect that names, short phrases and brief titles will not usually be given copyright protection. For example, in one case the judge felt that the authoress of *The Wombles* could not claim a monopoly in that name. In another case it was not possible to claim copyright over a single invented word. More recently the rock group Red Hot Chilli Peppers found it a struggle to establish copyright in their album title *Californication*, when a TV series used the same name.

Titles are often duplicated. The phrase 'The Eye of the Storm', for example, has been used by both Nobel prize-winning novelist, Patrick White, and thriller writer, Jack Higgins. As long as such words basically do not **pass-off** (disguise) – whether intentionally or not – one work as that of a different author, or mislead the public, there is usually no problem. Descriptive titles such as *Business Accounting* are safe. Be more wary of distinctive ones like *The Importance of Being Earnest*.

Similar passing-off considerations apply as regards any name under which you publish. There can also be restrictions on using any wording which is a trademark. (Surprisingly one self-publisher was recently reported as facing opposition for using 'Olympic' in a title, though ultimately no proceedings have been taken – at least at the time of writing. It remains to be seen how '2012 association rights' will impact in general.) It is increasingly common for titles and names to be trademarked (particularly when spin-off merchandising could be involved). David Bowie, for example, trademarked Ziggy Stardust. Providing that the criteria (usually involving 'distinctiveness') are met, registration need not be excessively complicated and can give protection. However, some expense can be involved and often the help of a trademark agent is obtained to assist in the procedure.

Longer extracts

Using longer extracts from another work in copyright can be dangerous without permission. In one case the taking of 600 words from a 200-page book was held to be an infringement. Even smaller amounts are unlikely to be tolerated by the courts if used in a rival work. They usually look askance at any work which competes and takes revenue away from something from which it 'borrows'. There is some flexibility if the use ranks as fair dealing.

Fair dealing

Firstly, fair dealing can cover **research and private study** for a non-commercial purpose, provided sufficient acknowledgement is given (except where impossible for reasons of practicality or other reasons). For example, you may resort to a reference library whilst working on an historical novel, and need to take notes from textbooks. This is likely to be a 'permitted act' (though regulations introduced in 2003 made the overall situation less clear and provided for 'fair compensation').

Writers are often more concerned, however, with fair dealing which covers **criticism, review and reporting of current events**. It is thought possibly to extend to more general areas such as illustrating a point and putting forward an argument.

Acknowledgement is required. Note that here criticism/review relates to the work, not comments on the author.

If fair dealing, you are allowed to take more of someone else's work. Just how much, only the courts can say for sure in each situation. Nevertheless, useful guidance was given through a statement by the Society of Authors and the Publishers Association some years ago in relation to fair dealing for criticism or review. The basis of this was:

◆ When taking a single prose extract, do not exceed 400 words.

◆ With a series of prose extracts, do not exceed 300 words for each and take no more than 800 words in all.

◆ In quoting poetry, do not use more than 40 lines and no more than a quarter of the whole poem in any event.

The criticism or review must relate to comments on the work (not, for example, be personal comments on the author).

Fair dealing does not apply to extracts used for an anthology. Then you must obtain express permission for **any** quotation of copyright material.

Similarly you should seek permission to quote song lyrics in copyright. Music companies can sometimes charge relatively high fees for this.

Poetry is especially vulnerable to being 'over-borrowed', as has been particularly highlighted by Wendy Cope's valiant efforts to

counter widespread ignorance of copyright law and stop
unauthorised use of poems on the Internet. A blatant example of
infringement occurred recently when a young performance poet,
Luke Wright, found his poems being read at events by someone
else as if they were their own work (which he acted promptly to
stop). As writers, we should always aim to respect restrictions on
others' work.

New developments

A recent government report (the *Gowers Review*) recommends new
exceptions to copyright restrictions, including:

◆ for the purpose of caricature, parody or pastiche;

◆ for creative, transformative or derivative works.

The second of these has raised concerns, such as with the Society
of Authors, which takes the view that it will be hard to distinguish
when a new work relies too heavily on an earlier one. Such issues
have led to much litigation in the US.

Paying fees

When permission is required, you may find you have to pay a fee.
The exact amount depends upon such factors as the author/
publisher concerned, the likely print run of your book and the
countries where it may be sold. The Society of Authors and the
Publishers Association, in consultation with the Association of
Authors' Agents, produce **guidance rates** on fees for quotation and
anthology use. Fees usually cover just one edition, so any other
later may require more payment.

Often you as author will have to bear such fees, but it is worth trying to negotiate on this with a publisher, who may pay or at least contribute to such expense. If you are ever asked to grant permission for quotation of your own work, you are also entitled to charge a fee. The Society of Authors can give guidance on appropriate rates applying from time to time.

Quoting accurately

If quoting from another's work, do so precisely. The courts have regarded it as extremely serious to miss out a single 'not' or to replace 'or' with 'and'.

ACKNOWLEDGING YOUR SOURCES

If you include a quotation either with permission or as fair dealing, you must give a sufficient acknowledgement which preferably should at least **identify the author and title** of the work from which it is taken. This can for example, be in your main text – perhaps in brackets – or as a footnote.

As regards sources generally, a traditional approach is to mention the author of the source by his last name, within your main text, and then to give full details of his work in a bibliography.

You can also insert a sweeping-up clause where you are not sure if you have used matters of **common knowledge** or not. This is useful to cover compilations, books of records/facts, or newspapers. An example is given in Figure 3.

Except where specifically acknowledged, the information included in this work is believed to be 'common knowledge' and its source is many and varied. Whilst there has been no verbatim use of copy, it is possible that some has been gleaned from publications such as (*insert names of publications, authors and publishers*) and this is gratefully acknowledged.

Fig. 3. Sample clause relating to general sources.

AVOIDING PLAGIARISM

What is plagiarism?

Plagiarism is not a technical legal term. It derives from the Latin for 'kidnapping'. It commonly means the appropriating of another's ideas or work. It is often used by writers and publishers loosely to cover not only straightforward copying but also the 'stealing' of basic ideas and plots. (There is, however, an academic argument against breach of copyright being within the legal definition of theft.)

How can you prevent being plagiarised?

As you have seen, copyright is in the written form, rather than general ideas. It is also widely felt that there is a finite number of plots (boy meets girls, rags to riches and so on) with permutations. Therefore it is difficult to obtain legal protection from this form of plagiarism, without very close similarity being involved, and being able to show that a combination or series of dramatic events has been taken from your own work. Case law indicates that you have to show quite close copying – not just use of stock characters and incidents. If the other author can prove they had no knowledge of your work, this gives them a defence.

Other sanctions can exist, such as bad press and damage to literary reputation. The standing of the great short story writer, Katherine Mansfield, was affected for a time by such suggestions regarding similarity between one of her stories and one by Chekhov. (She may even have suffered blackmail over this.)

Hitting on the same idea as someone else frequently happens. There seem to be trends in creativity.

In protecting your own original ideas/information from less coincidental circumstances, the law of confidence can help in certain situations.

The law of confidence
This is often used by inventors or designers to protect confidential information to safeguard commercial 'know-how'. It can sometimes help in situations where discussions need to be confidential, such as between author and publisher, or taking a programme idea to a television producer. However, it is unlikely to protect an unsolicited idea offered to a publisher you have never dealt with before.

One example of use of this law arises from a case concerning certain actresses who described a developed idea for a programme about a female rock band to a script writer, who passed it to a producer and TV company. They were successful in court when the programme was later developed without allowing all of them a part in it.

Although lawyers agree that this law exists, there is an academic squabble over what type it is. It may be:

♦ a right implied into a contract;

♦ a tort (civil wrong) preventing disclosure of anything confidential;

♦ a property right; *or*

♦ based upon equitable principles of good faith.

The last is the most probable. Under this, someone in possession of confidential information is regarded as like a trustee and has a duty not to let that information pass into the wrong hands nor to exploit it without permission. To get protection from this law, you are on strong ground if you can show that:

♦ the type of information involved is usually treated as confidential;

♦ the information was revealed in confidential circumstances;

♦ it was then used without your authority to your detriment;

♦ the ideas involved were original, not too vague and with commercial attraction.

That said, some case law (mainly regarding trade secrets and employment, but with more general implications) has unfortunately indicated that the courts could take a more restrictive approach to breach of confidence claims. It is difficult – but not impossible – to show breach of confidentiality.

Using this law

The law may apply where you have a close relationship with a publisher or an agent and allow them to be privy to your ideas for a new book. Certain steps can be taken to strengthen any case you might have.

◆ Make it clear in any contact, correspondence, 'pitching', discussions or negotiations that you regard the subject matter as confidential and try to ensure this is accepted on both sides.

◆ Write down your full idea (oral ideas are more difficult to protect), and consider lodging a copy with a third party like your bank/solicitor to show you thought of this and when.

◆ Keep a record of the time you spent developing the idea.

◆ Keep copies of correspondence and records of meetings, discussions, etc. (Reconstructed diaries have sometimes been used in court as evidence.)

◆ Get an express clause in any contract to the effect that relevant discussions are confidential (see Chapter 6).

Legal remedies under the law of confidence are similar to those regarding copyright (see Chapter 2). However, there is never any automatic right to an injunction, so even if you are successful, the court may only award damages.

Could you be a plagiarist?

You will hopefully follow the guidelines given to help you avoid breach of copyright. Also be careful to avoid too much similarity in general to any other work.

There have been instances of whole books being 'borrowed', with a few factors like names and location changed. Underneath, the original was still well-recognisable. No writer worth his/her salt would stoop to such unethical practice – at least knowingly.

There is some recognition of the phenomena of 'subconscious copying'. We all imbibe influences from what we read. The genius of T. S. Eliot's poetry exploited this to full effect. It could be that an author reads a book decades earlier and then reproduces it later believing it to be original. Unfortunately, it is very difficult to take measures to control your subconscious. At least be aware of the main works within your genre and steer clear of close similarity.

The dangers and potential fall-out were shown recently in reports of a young novelist who signed a six-figure two-book contract, only to find her career blighted when similarities between her work and that in the novels of others came to light.

PHOTOCOPYING

Photocopying material which is in copyright is technically restricted. You are generally allowed to copy a small portion of a book for a non-commercial purpose, for your own research and private study. This falls within fair dealing.

The restrictions are important when it comes to voluminous copying. (Otherwise writers, including you, would lose potential royalties.) The **Copyright Licensing Agency** (**CLA**) was set up to help control the situation. It issues licences to such bodies as educational authorities, business concerns, and government departments in return for a fee. The **Newspaper Licensing Agency** (**NLA**) deals with the copying of newspaper reports and articles. Regulations introduced in 2003 affect commercial copying. Guidance on this can be found at www.cla.co.uk.

As a book author, you should receive an appropriate share of the revenues collected. These can be remunerative for frequently consulted non-fiction. Payment in respect of magazines and journals, however, usually all goes to the publisher.

BEING AWARE OF DATA PROTECTION

The Data Protection Act 1998 could affect you. It covers computerised and manual records, and applies where:

- a data controller (possibly you);

- processes personal data;

- relating to data subjects.

Personal data includes details from which someone can be identified. In general terms, a data subject can be any individual, for example a research participant, a contractor or a customer, who can be identified from the data or the data in connection with other available information.

The legislation lays down principles and places an emphasis on **notification, accuracy, fairness** and **subjects having access** to data held about them. If there is a breach, they can complain to the **Information Commissioner**. The matter can also be taken to court, where compensation may be given.

At the time of writing, the Information Commissioner can give only relatively limited redress. However, there has recently been increased concern in this area following loss of a disc by HM Revenue and Customs, together with other instances of lost data in the public and private sectors. The present Information Commissioner has requested a **major change in enforcement powers**. His proposals include a **new criminal offence** linked to the duty to comply with Data Protection Act principles, but it would be a defence to show you had exercised **due diligence**. Also included is a power to impose **civil penalties** instead. It remains to be seen whether the Information Commissioner's requests will be implemented. Whatever happens, there has to be a rising awareness of the **importance of compliance**.

Data can include information in databases, spreadsheet files, electronic records or paper format for later computer input, and in manual systems, as part of a **relevant filing system**. Case law suggests that a relevant filing system means something structured so that specific information about an individual can be readily located.

There are two sorts of data:

◆ **personal** e.g. names and addresses;

◆ **sensitive** e.g. ethnic origin, political opinions, religious beliefs, health factors.

To help you stay on the right side of data protection provisions, you can obtain free guidance and leaflets from the Information Commissioner's Office (see addresses at the back of this book). These explain the principles to be followed, such as how personal information is gathered and stored, and for how long (with emphasis on not keeping data longer than necessary). Be aware of the rights of data subjects, including the right to object to the direct marketing of personal data.

Case law has suggested that data protection legislation could, in certain circumstances, stop commercial exploitation of someone's image without consent, and therefore enhance privacy law (see also Chapter 4). Because UK law has no 'image rights' as such, other law is sometimes used, like false endorsement and passing-off, as well as data protection.

♦ Beware companies asking you to register and pay them a fee under data protection regulations.

Writers have sometimes been targeted by such scams (see also www.dpr.gov.uk/dontbemisled.htm).

The Freedom of Information Act 2000 is unlikely to impose any burden upon you. It basically allows people access to relevant personal or environmental information (under the Environmental Information Regulations), held by public authorities, such as hospitals or local authorities. Bear it in mind, if you ever need such details, for example in research for an article.

Journalists are finding FoIA requests an increasingly useful tool in some circumstances. Any request must:

♦ be in writing (letter, email or fax);

♦ give your name and address (email or postal);

♦ outline the information sought.

A fee may be payable. Public authorities usually have their publication scheme available online, which often includes answers to routine questions. Requests should be answered within 20 working days unless exemptions apply, for example where health and safety could be compromised or disclosure is prohibited by law.

CASE STUDIES

Liz carries out a study

Liz is commissioned by a magazine to write on women's experiences in relation to maternity rights.

She interviews several women, recording their names, addresses, details of employment and the maternity benefits and overall treatment which they received. In her article, Liz states no names but describes their situations and draws overall conclusions. Each woman's permission has been obtained for this.

Liz must be mindful of the Data Protection Act. It is the information received by her which is relevant to this – not her article.

Her records are likely to be held on a 'relevant filing system' and Liz needs to observe the regulations. She should contact the Information Commissioner's Office, for free leaflets and guidance. Whilst the original unwieldy registration system has gone, Liz may still have to give **notification** of information she holds and what she intends to do with it. (There is usually no need to notify, if personal data only is processed for such as advertising, marketing and public relations.) Liz may need the women's written consent, especially if her files contain sensitive information, such as on their race or religion.

Bill backs it up with statistics

In writing the biography, Bill comes across a recent publication which gives statistics illustrating the average life-span and health of Victorian males.

Bill wishes to use these statistics to illustrate the expectations and quality of life which the subject of his biography would have. He intends to include a table from the text concerned in his own work.

Although Bill is using facts, over which there is usually no copyright, the table is the result of skill and labour by the writer and it will almost certainly be copyright. Using the whole format is unlikely to be within fair dealing. The law concerning databases could also be relevant. Bill should obtain consent, through approaching the publisher's Permissions Department at an early stage. He may have to pay a fee.

If Bill has not yet found a publisher, he could leave his application until later. His eventual publisher may possibly agree to pay the cost (or at least fund this for now, then later recover it from royalties) or this suggested inclusion may be edited out anyway. It may still be useful for him to try to obtain an estimate of the permission cost at this stage.

Daniel's great idea

Daniel is negotiating with an independent TV company on his proposed sit-com. It centres upon the catering corps and the 'ups and downs' in the life of an eccentric army cook.

As far as Daniel is aware, nothing on these lines has been done before. He has developed the idea, discussed it with the producer (who has indicated that Daniel will be commissioned for the script) and written a first draft. The TV company discuss this with him, then suddenly tell him they have decided not to pursue the project. It is not until sometime later that Daniel learns that they are continuing with it in the same format, using his plot and characters, but have taken on a new writer.

Daniel may have a claim under the law of confidence, because he discussed his idea in circumstances of confidentiality. He should strongly protest. If necessary, he should threaten proceedings (which case law suggests could potentially award him substantial damages), and negotiate to be reinstated as script writer, if he so wishes, or otherwise try to obtain an out-of-court settlement (see Chapters 7 and 8).

SUMMARY

◆ In drawing upon research always re-work this, going direct to original sources, and devising your own form of presentation.

◆ To quote from a work which is in copyright, the only foolproof way is to obtain permission from the copyright owner.

◆ Short phrases, names and titles can, however, sometimes be used without permission.

◆ If you are 'fair dealing', no permission is required but stay within the guidance given in this chapter and give an acknowledgement.

◆ Acknowledge your sources with at least the author's name and the title.

◆ Stress confidentiality of proposals with publishers/agents and anyone else with whom you enter discussions.

◆ Bear in mind the Data Protection provisions as regards any information you hold.

POINTS TO CONSIDER

1. List the circumstances when it might be said that 'facts can be copyright'.

2. Consider whether you could adopt a pen name of Joe K. Rowling.

3. In your novel, you want to quote twelve lines of a modern poem. Consider which circumstances might make it advisable to seek permission.

4

Avoiding Libel

Beyond the redemption of the courts.

> Diplock LJ's comment on the law of libel
> in *Slim* v. *Daily Telegraph Ltd* (1968)

WHAT IS LIBEL?

Libel is one part of the law of defamation. The other part is slander. Broadly speaking, libel is written, slander is spoken. Both involve statements which are **defamatory** – basically insulting to reputation.

Playing the game

To understand libel properly, you must look at the legal rules involved. 'Rules' is an apt term. They are devious and elaborate. It is no surprise that a board game was marketed under the title 'Libel'. A well-known *Coronation Street* actor was involved in the promotion, himself fresh from successful litigation.

Before judge and jury

Defamation is a tort, i.e. a civil wrong as opposed to a crime. In rare circumstances, libel can be a crime, such as if it could lead to a breach of the peace, or if it creates an offence such as treason, sedition or blasphemous libel. (However, recent proceedings brought regarding a television production of *Jerry Springer: the Opera* failed and it seems less likely that blasphemous libel will continue as an offence.)

Writers are mainly troubled by the civil version, for which a slandered or libelled person may sue. Traditionally, a judge and jury are involved, which is one reason why it can be expensive.

The expense is a deterrent as regards those who might wish to sue you over something you have written. If you are sued, however, the financial risk to you is high. In the past, juries have sometimes stipulated massive amounts of damages to send out a message as well as give compensation. A few years ago, certain libel damages awarded to Elton John were cut. The Court of Appeal gave guidelines it was hoped would lead to more consistency and perhaps prevent excessive awards. Some cases have indicated a trend towards lesser awards (though large awards are still not unknown). Courts will normally discount damages where a prompt admission of liability is made. The **Defamation Act 1996** also aimed to help reduce legal costs by such means as introducing a fast-track procedure for relatively straightforward claims under £10,000, so that in certain circumstances the matter can be dealt with summarily by a judge alone. The overhaul of the court system a few years ago also reduced costs. Law firms often take libel cases on a 'no win, no fee' or conditional fee basis, sometimes with an additional 'success fee' and usually with higher fees charged overall. (There have recently been moves towards agreement to limit/cap fees, in some circumstances.) Nevertheless, the pecuniary penalty for libel can be substantial. You may have to pay the other party's costs too, in addition to being saddled with an injunction preventing future publication of the work involved.

HOW FAR CAN YOU GO?

In what you write

Whilst freedom of speech is included in the Human Rights Act 1998 (incorporating the European Convention on Human Rights into UK law), defamation is one type of law setting boundaries on what you can say. Writers are obviously more at risk from libel rather than from slander. Less obvious is what this includes. Whereas slander is mainly speech in an unrecorded form, libel can be through not only literature, but also work broadcast on radio and television, the performance of a play or illustrations.

Therefore **any form your work takes** is capable of containing libel. That can include electronic forms, with e-mail usage and websites increasingly at risk.

A recent case held that **postings on a website** alleging greed and dishonest behaviour justified legal redress. Damages have been ordered for abrasive and defamatory comments on an **online forum**. Research by legal publishers, Sweet & Maxwell, suggests that a growing number of libel cases are being based upon comments posted on the Internet via **blogs** or **message boards**. Internet service providers could find themselves in trouble, if they fail to investigate a complaint and many tend to take such grievances seriously, especially if raised through a solicitor.

In what you do with it

For there to be any claim, material **has to be published**. This includes self-publishing, small press, competition anthologies, writers' circle magazines and merely showing your work to any third party. The reading aloud of written work at a writers' workshop is sufficient.

A book involves a series of 'publications' for legal purposes:

- the author submitting the work to the publisher;

- the work being passed to the printer;

- the work being passed to the distributor;

- the work being passed down the chain to the bookseller;

- the work reaching the public.

The middle-men cannot usually be sued for libel, providing they were careful and knew nothing of it. Internet providers may have a similar potential defence (though if made aware of defamatory material through such as a complaint, may have to remove it). Those at the top of the chain – you, your editor and your publisher – are always at risk.

In what you say

There is no libel unless the work is defamatory, i.e. likely to bring hatred, ridicule or contempt upon someone. For this, it must harm someone's reputation **or** cause that person to be shunned or avoided, in the opinion of right-thinking members of the community. This is why a jury is traditionally required at any hearing. It represents 'right-thinking' and gives its opinion on the effect of the work.

Therefore references such as to dishonesty, immorality or insanity will be potentially libellous. So too will suggestions of someone having an infectious disease or being bankrupt, because these things tend to cause a person (rightly or wrongly) to be shunned by others.

In how you say it

Libel need not be expressed. It can also be by implication (or what the law terms 'innuendo'). A waxwork was once found defamatory because nearby was a 'Chamber of Horrors' sign. Watch not only what you say, but how you say it.

In whom you say it about

It is commonly thought safe to libel the dead. It is true that their right to sue cannot be 'inherited' by anyone else. But think first about whether 'talking ill of the dead' could reflect on the deceased's relatives. For example, a statement that the late Mr A. Aardvark was a bigamist could implicate his last known wife in a similar offence.

It is usually safe to be derogatory of organs of central government and local authorities, as they cannot sue for libel. Implied criticism, however, of particular officers would lead to action. If your motives are malicious, you could also be sued for 'injurious falsehood'.

Generalisations over a large class of people are reasonably risk-free; for example, 'All editors are idiots' – unless there was an implication within the context that your remark was directed at a certain individual. A case where someone objected to a dictionary definition of the word 'jew' failed because he could not show that it referred to him in particular. (This was before modern race relations legislation.)

PREVENTING LEGAL ACTION

The net of libel stretches wide. You must take care to escape from it when first committing your ideas to paper.

Fiction writers may feel that they can hide behind a disclaimer, such as:

> 'All characters in this book are imaginary and any resemblance to any living person is coincidental.'

This carries little legal force. Many publishers do not bother to include it. The court looks at whether the effect of the work was that someone was defamed. Lack of intention to do so or 'coincidental' bad luck is irrelevant to liability (though can help a defence – see later).

Let us consider circumstances which could create a risk.

Pure coincidence

This might be termed 'the nightmare scenario'. You create a brilliant portrayal of a main character. He or she may be villainous, debauched, stupid or barking mad – but definitely imaginary. Yet upon publication, the creation appears in the flesh, like the wrath of Frankenstein, threatening proceedings. An old case established there was **liability even where the author did not know of the existence of the person he described**. This concerned a humorous article on a Mr Artemus Jones in Dieppe, accompanied by a lady who was not his wife. In the early twentieth century this was seen as defamatory of a London barrister, who, yes, was called Artemus Jones.

There is a defence available (see later). Your publisher will resent the expense and inconvenience of it and may look to the contract to make you bear any cost involved (see Chapter 5). Basic care should be taken at the outset not to make unintended reference to a living person.

Simple procedural checks can be taken. Suppose, for example, your villain is a fraudulent property surveyor. It is relatively easy to telephone the RICS information desk to check that no one of the same name exists on their register. If your character is identified as coming from or operating within a narrow geographical area, then consult telephone directories in the library. The Internet may also be a useful tool. Even if such checks are not foolproof, your carrying them out can help your defence later.

No coincidence

This is where, as a fiction writer, you really are to blame – not so much for intentionally maligning someone, but if you do not bring sufficient creativity into your portrayal to disguise the fact.

Many writers do, of course, start with those people and relationships around them. For some of the greatest, such as Proust and D. H. Lawrence, there seems to have been no other way. Not to do so may be safer, but how much inspiration would be lost as a result? General advice is to write about what you know. Does this have to be confined to flattering your subjects? Fortunately fiction writers aim to create more than a reflection of the actual. In drawing upon life, it is necessary both artistically and legally to adapt and evolve a character.

You should, of course, change names. The use of an unlikely name, however, affords feeble protection if a real person is still recognisable from the text. You should **significantly alter names and background** (even if you feel that no one has been defamed – a jury may disagree).

If the integrity of the work will not suffer, then **consider changing, for example, age and gender**, and including an imagined quirk or two. This is not to say that some similarity to well-known figures cannot be very saleable, as with the Hollywood echoes of Jacqueline Susann's *Valley of the Dolls*. (Strong denials were given, and sales seemed to soar correspondingly.) Fiction must, however, in general, be sufficiently removed from life **so that a sensible reader cannot be expected to connect it with a particular person**.

You could maintain that your readers will not be aware of the actual people upon whom it was based, and therefore no one can claim their reputation has suffered. The law has thought of that one, and **assumes** that 'a sensible reader' will have **knowledge of special facts** which could connect the characters with life.

You could also argue, 'No one agreed with me anyway.' In law it is irrelevant that no reader believed your words to be true. If your writing suggests something defamatory of a person, then that is libel.

DEFENDING LEGAL ACTION

If proceedings are threatened or commenced, there are several potential defences. (It is also useful to note that the **Defamation Act 1996** reduced the limitation period to bring libel claims to just one year, subject to the court's rarely used discretion to extend this.)

'The truth, the whole truth'

It does not normally matter what you say, as long as it is factually true. **Justification** is a complete defence to libel (usually even if the writer acted out of malice). Mistake, however, is not. Stating something **you believe** to be true, even upon good authority, will leave you **liable** if it proves to be **incorrect**.

Ensure the accuracy of sources and keep these available as evidence. The burden of proving that something is true is on you. The court presumes that anything defamatory is untrue until you convince it otherwise. *Private Eye* (no stranger to libel litigation) was caught out when it falsely alleged that the wife of the Yorkshire Ripper had agreed to sell her story to *The Daily Mail* for £25,000. They were ordered to pay a cool £600,000 – but after appeal, the matter was settled at a cold comfort price of £60,000.

A more recent case involved a famous hypnotherapist, who successfully sued a newspaper group for wrongly implying that his degree was of little worth and granted merely for money. The burden of proof was on the respondent to show that the sting of the words was substantially true.

'Fair enough'

The other defence which may be available is **fair comment**. This exists to protect freedom of speech. It is particularly relevant to journalists expressing opinion upon **matters of pubic interest**. It also covers critics of books, theatre, film, TV and radio.

In fact, the comment need not be 'fair' in the usual sense. It must simply be what the law regards as 'honest', i.e. **based upon correct facts** and an opinion which an honest man could hold, however prejudiced and obstinate he might be!

The comment must **not be motivated by malice**. The court found a review in *Punch* not fair comment because of ill-will between the reviewer and the author. It may be better for a critic to decline work concerning an artist for whom there is evidence that he holds personal animosity.

'Sorry, honest!'

A special defence is available if you can show your **words were used 'innocently'**, and you did not intend to libel anyone.

The Defamation Act 1996 allows you to make an 'offer to make amends'. In broad terms, this is

◆ to make a suitable correction and sufficient apology;

◆ to publish the correction and apology in a reasonable and practicable manner;

◆ to pay compensation and costs.

If the amount to be paid cannot be agreed with the claimant, it can be fixed by a judge. The offer should be **in writing** and stated to be an offer made **under section 2 of the Defamation Act 1996**. It should be stated whether it is a 'qualified offer'. This is where your offer, rather than being in relation to the statement generally, is in relation to a specific defamatory meaning which you accept that the statement conveys. You must give details of the defamatory meaning to which the offer relates. You can make a qualified offer to cover those defamatory statements you claim to have made innocently, but apply another defence to the remainder.

If the offer is rejected but not withdrawn, you can elect to use it as a defence, but usually you will not then be able to use any other defence. The offer may also be relied upon in mitigation (which helps reduce any damages), whether or not used as a defence.

It can help to support your 'innocence' in the face of any challenge if you keep early drafts through which a character was developed. Some writers invent a whole biography (as recommended by many tutors). Most of this never features in the main text, but assists the writer to give depth to his protagonist. These notes can show how you created your fiction independently of any real life influences.

Although such evidence is not conclusive and could be fabricated after the event, a court may not automatically doubt your integrity, so such material can provide corroboration if you are challenged.

Some privilege

Privilege is a defence which can be particularly relevant to journalists. **Absolute privilege** can for example sometimes cover fair, accurate and contemporaneous reports of judicial proceedings in this country. **Qualified privilege** applies only where there is no malice and may cover things such as fair and accurate media reports of certain proceedings, public meetings and other events. A House of Lords case indicated that the factors which the courts may take into account include:

◆ seriousness of the allegations;

◆ nature of the information and extent to which it is of public concern;

◆ source;

◆ status of the information;

◆ steps taken to verify its accuracy;

- urgency involved;

- whether comment was sought from the person concerned;

- whether the gist of that side of the story was given;

- tone/style used;

- circumstances of publication.

This is known as the Reynolds defence'. Case law has indicated that this basically boils down to publishing in a responsible manner. A recent Court of Appeal case has shown that this can now be used by authors as well as journalists. However, the court made clear that greater care would be expected of book authors as they have the benefit of a longer timescale for publication.

CASE STUDIES

Liz and the naughty vicar

In a draft novel, Liz introduces a lecherous clergyman who pursues her married heroine. She has given him the unlikely name of Damien Blennerhassett, and set her story in a fictionalised Cotswold village. A certain Reverend David Blenerhausset from Chipping Camden has now complained.

The similarity in names, coupled with the locality, places Liz on thin ice. The depiction of the character in her novel is potentially libellous. Even if no reader is likely to know the real Reverend Blenerhausset or believe him capable of the conduct of Liz's protagonist, this will not alter the position. It only matters that the words were capable of harming his reputation. However, provided Liz knew nothing of the real vicar (and there appears to be no evidence to suggest that she could have known of him) and was not reckless, it may then be possible to placate Reverend Blenerhausset with an appropriate offer to make amends.

Bill tells it like it was

In the biography, Bill feels that he must recount certain 'indiscretions' of his otherwise virtuous Victorian. Evidence for these comes from a grandson whom Bill has interviewed in the course of his research. Bill intends to report the stories told by the relative (which have been handed down through the family), and to add his own comments that he is sceptical as to their full validity.

Bill need have no concern as to how this may affect the deceased's reputation (the old adage that you cannot libel the dead). He should, however, consider the nature of the 'indiscretions' and whether stating them could affect anyone else. For example, could they imply that a living person is illegitimate?

The fact that Bill is simply recording statements made by the grandson would not prevent Bill from being sued. Anyone who openly repeats libel in effect publicises it for legal purposes. Bill might have the defence of justification if the reports are true. It is unlikely he would be able to prove this as he himself seems to doubt them. Furthermore, in commenting on his own scepticism, Bill might imply that the grandson is a liar. Therefore, Bill may be safest to leave out the grandson's information, until he knows that it is more than mere 'hearsay' and he has factual evidence to back it up.

Bill should exercise a degree of care in his methods of collecting information. Although hopefully this would never apply to Bill, the **Protection from Harassment Act 1997** introduced certain criminal offences and the statutory tort of harassment. Following the death of Princess Diana, there was renewed focus on conduct which could amount to harassment, leading to a new Press Complaints Commission Code of Practice. This recently led to a finding against a newspapers for publishing a rumour of a celebrity's pregnancy before her 12-week scan, without consent. **Privacy rights** are gaining more recognition, especially as Article 8 of the European Convention on Human Rights covers respect for private and family life. These were enhanced further by a recent decision of the European Court of Human Rights, concerning Princess Caroline of Monaco. Recent cases here (notably involving celebrities like Naomi Campbell, David and Victoria Beckham, Michael Douglas and Catherine Zeta-Jones, Sienna Miller and also the author, J.K. Rowling) have mainly centred on photographs.

Privacy rights have to be balanced against freedom of expression. Case law shows the courts are feeling their way in this, as the new law develops, but with privacy often upheld. A recent example is a case involving a book written by a former friend of a Canadian folk singer. An injunction was given stopping publication because details in the book breached the singer's privacy.

Daniel makes a point

Daniel wishes to dramatise some of his experience in the army, involving a particular officer whom he feels (but cannot prove) abused his power.

Daniel must proceed very carefully. He would be wise to change the officer's name, age, exact rank and background. For example, he could alter geographical and family origins. He must also make sure that there can be no close identification through association with other characters. Therefore they too must be fictionalised to some extent. In drawing upon his experience, he must also change the exact details of what happened.

Daniel might also consider taking out libel insurance, but this can be expensive. (Sometimes, authors can arrange to be covered on their publisher's insurance.)

SUMMARY

♦ Make checks that the names which you choose for your characters are not those of similar persons in real-life, for example, in the same profession or geographical area.

♦ If you draw upon life, change names and background. Consider also altering age and gender and adding different characteristics.

♦ Ensure your sources of factual information are reliable and keep records of them.

♦ If in doubt, leave it out.

♦ You can insert a disclaimer like the one set out earlier in this chapter. Bear in mind that, whilst it does no legal harm, it carries little strength.

POINTS TO CONSIDER

1. Consider whether the following suggestions could be defamatory:

   – that a local council is 'on the take';

   – that a famous actor is to join a cloistered religious sect;

   – that a certain businessman is effective but ruthless.

2. You wish to write a wartime novel, which refers to several prominent figures of the time. The plot involves treachery on the part of one of Churchill's aides. When might you have to guard against libel? List the steps you would take to do so.

3. An arch-rival gives a slating and incorrect review of your latest book. In what circumstances can you sue?

5

Entering a Contract

This kindness I will show –
Go with me to a notary, seal me there
Your single bond.

(Merchant of Venice, Act I, Scene iii, Shakespeare)

UNDERSTANDING BASIC CONTRACT LAW

A contract need not always be a signed document. There is, however, a lawyer's saying that 'a verbal contract is not worth the paper it's written on.' The golden rule is **get it in writing**.

What is the vital 'it'? To understand this, you must appreciate the legal basis of any binding agreement. This can be usefully illustrated in relation to **dealings with a magazine**, which you will consider in this chapter. In Chapter 6 you will look at contracts with book publishers, where there is likely to be a more formal document involved.

What is required for a binding contract?

The following are the basic 'ingredients' required.

Offer and acceptance
This can be when you offer your manuscript, which the publication accepts. Alternatively, it is arguable and more likely that your submission is only 'an invitation to treat'. The publication then offers to publish it at a fee, which you accept. Similarly with commissions, you accept work offered by the editor on specified terms.

Consideration

This is an exchange of promises (or an act in exchange for a promise) worth something to each party. It is your allowing publication in exchange for the promise of payment. Forgoing payment or accepting a nominal sum – as with some small press arrangements – can still be classed as consideration because you gain the benefit of the work being published. You might, for example, be willing to forgo payment for an article on the basis that it will also give publicity to you and/or your latest book.

Intention to create legal relations

This is usually implied in the commercial context of publishing.

Capacity

In general you must be over eighteen, sane and sober when you enter a contract (otherwise special rules apply).

Legality

This is unlikely to affect you. The courts can refuse to enforce any contract which is contrary to legislation or public policy. A contract killing is an extreme example.

Consensus ad idem

This lawyer's Latin means that there must be an agreement without anything, such as misrepresentation, to undermine it. You will cover this area in Chapter 7.

Privity of contract

You have to be a party to a contract to enforce it. Generally, third parties cannot enforce claims under it, though legislation has impacted on this traditional position in some circumstances.

STIPULATING TERMS

Binding terms

To be enforceable, the terms of any contract must be **certain**. If a magazine uses an imprecise phrase like 'publication subject to space availability', this might be void for uncertainty with no obligation on them to use your work. Aim to **get conditions spelt out**. If the magazine's letter is vague, ensure your reply clarifies the arrangements agreed, such as delivery date.

Bear in mind that the courts would normally look at the contract as a whole and give any words used in it their ordinary and natural meaning, unless there is a **specific definition** in the contract. Sometimes they take into account the general conduct of the parties to work out their intentions. If terms are not clear, there is a **risk that the entire contract could be declared invalid**, though more often than not the courts just rule that **any unclear provision is invalid**.

Make clear any agreed fee and when payment becomes due. Some magazines pay on acceptance, but on publication is more common. Try to agree payment within seven days of the proposed publication date, time to be of the essence. This will help avoid any 'reasonable time' which could be implied by law, and which is a recipe for debate and late payment. If work is commissioned, try to agree a fixed payment date, so you are paid by then even if publication is postponed.

Other terms which you may try to include are that:

◆ you grant only First British serial rights (see Chapter 6);

◆ you can approve changes, if practicable;

◆ (to avoid any doubt) you will be credited;

◆ any deadline and word count requirement on commissioned work.

If the publication wants to publish online as well, the fee should reflect this, especially if readers have to pay to download.

Online publication tends to be worldwide, so you would be unlikely to be able to offer serial rights elsewhere. Consider whether you might therefore want to impose a time limit such as two years on any online version.

Syndication rights

Magazines often seek these, especially with commissioned articles. You should ask for a share (perhaps 50%) of any income from syndication, to be paid within one month of receipt by the publication. Try to avoid giving away full copyright, as you lose any say in changes made and the right to be credited or the chance to receive any further payment on further use of the work. If the publication demands assignment, then try to agree that after a certain time, you will be allowed to use the work elsewhere, crediting the magazine with original publication.

Photocopying rights

Income from photocopying writers' work that is still in copyright is generally **handled by ALCS** (see also Chapter 2). Its stated aims are to protect and promote writers' rights by:

◆ encouraging the establishment of collective licensing schemes;

♦ enhancing awareness of copyright issues, so writers maximise their income;

♦ ensuring fees from licensing schemes are properly collected and distributed.

You can help them to help you by joining and registering with them (free to members of the National Union of Journalists, Society of Authors and Writers' Guild). Since 1997, ALCS has collected photocopying royalties for journals and magazines within the UK and overseas. (You may find, as I have, that it is a pleasant surprise through this to discover copying and interest in your work in countries you had not expected.)

To register your articles with ALCS:

♦ access the Members' Area of the website www.alcs.co.uk and submit details online; *or*

♦ download a magazine/journal articles from the 'Download Forms' section of the website and send it to ALCS (see addresses at the back of this book); *or*

♦ request that a magazine/journal form be posted to you to complete by emailing membership@alcs.co.uk or telephoning 020 7264 5700; *or*

♦ send ALCS a summary of your articles and your details.

You can claim royalties back to January 2004. The articles concerned have to have been published in the UK and the publication must have an eight-digit ISSN identification number. In addition to this information, try to give the titles of the magazine and article with approximate word count, publication date and the names of any co-authors.

Confirming matters in writing

Editors may not have time to send letters repeating telephone conversations, but there is nothing to stop you sending a note or email 'just to confirm our discussion' (keeping a copy). It must embody the terms agreed. You cannot unilaterally impose terms. You could devise a standard letter on your PC, so that despite deadlines, you can find a few minutes to fill in the blanks and get this posted/faxed/emailed. It will also enhance your business-like image to the editor.

Example – 'half-commissions'

The need for written confirmation is underlined by the following examples. One freelance found that an editor whom she trusted suddenly refused to print or pay for an article he had verbally commissioned. She suspected that he had accidentally double-commissioned it. That should have been his problem, but there was nothing in writing. A major weekly magazine also changed its mind on a star interview, which she had gone to lengths to obtain. Fortunately this commission was confirmed in correspondence. After a few hints at proceedings, she received payment.

BENEFITING FROM A CONTRACT

A potentially enforceable contract is a deterrent against unscrupulous editors, who may want features and stories available without giving any commitment to using them.

A legally binding contract also is the basis of your getting paid. It is the springboard for taking appropriate action if you do not (see Chapter 8).

◆ Bear in mind also that the requirements for a contract work both ways. Be careful that your own correspondence does not provide these essential ingredients, if you are merely negotiating and do not yet wish to be bound. If in any doubt, you can head your letters '**subject to contract**' and make it clear that you are not entering into any binding agreement at this stage.

CASE STUDIES

The following case studies are based on just one of the writers whose paths you have been following, Liz. She frequently deals with magazines and has been successful at placing stories and articles with them.

Liz loses an editor

For several years, Liz has sold stories to a particular magazine fiction editor. She recently received an acceptance for her latest stating 'our usual terms apply'. She later received a letter saying that the editor had left, editorial policy had changed and Liz's fiction was no longer suitable.

Liz can do nothing to compel the magazine to take future stories but should press for the latest to be published/paid for. She must show a contract for this based on the acceptance letter. 'Our usual terms apply' could be too uncertain. If, however, Liz has earlier correspondence clearly showing 'a previous course of dealings' she may be able to claim that specific terms are implied. These might relate to a standard fee and payment arrangement.

A change of editor does not usually negate any contract. The editor here was acting as a representative of the magazine company, not in a personal capacity.

Liz gets an interview

Liz is approached by a magazine that has been impressed with
articles she has written on finding the right childcare provision,
partly drawing upon her own experience. The publication wants to
interview her on this. Before she agrees, Liz asks whether this will
be in person or over the telephone and whether a fee will be paid.
As is often the case, no fee is offered, but a telephone interview is
arranged for a time convenient for Liz. Liz stipulates that she
wants to be properly credited, with mention made of her website
(on which her services as a freelance writer are advertised). The
magazine is happy to do this. Liz also asks whether she can see the
copy article before it goes to print. The interviewer is unable to
guarantee this but at least says that 'if it proves feasible', a copy
will be emailed for her to look over before publication. Overall, Liz
decides she is happy to give the interview, as it will provide good
publicity for her. She sends an email to confirm the terms agreed.

Liz knows her rights

Liz has submitted several articles to a particular journal. In each
case, she confirmed terms agreed in writing, including that she
was offering first UK serial rights. Later she discovers that her
articles have been reproduced online in various places. She
contacts the journal, which admits that it authorised this but
protests that it only accepts full copyright, as per its standard
practice. Liz refers it to her written confirmation, which does not
accord with this and argues that the journal made a wrong
assumption. A recent legal case involved similar circumstances and
the court confirmed the principle that the author retains copyright
unless it has been expressly assigned in writing. Liz is therefore on
strong ground to insist on recompense, such as a decent share of
the income from the further publication.

SUMMARY

◆ Always get an agreement recorded in writing.

◆ With magazines and newspapers, this will usually be through correspondence.

◆ Specify all main terms, such as publication, payment and date when this is due.

◆ Be as precise as possible in stating the terms agreed.

◆ Register with ALCS to obtain income derived from photocopying rights.

POINTS TO CONSIDER

1. List the main items required to make an agreement into a binding contract.

2. In relation to your own work, think what are the main terms you should make clear before agreeing to meet an editor's deadline.

3. Devise a letter to a magazine confirming a commission for an article, including the main points to evidence a contract.

6

Negotiating a Publishing Contract

When you arrive at the wonderful position of having a publisher who wants to take your book, it is easy to overlook important details in your excitement. This is the time when you need to remain calm and clear-headed. The terms upon which your publishing contract are agreed may be vital to your future career as a writer. Consider also seeking professional help.

DO YOU NEED AN AGENT?

This is an important question when it comes to book contracts particularly for fiction. It may already be answered. You may have been represented by an agent in placing your manuscript. He or she will continue to act on your behalf in negotiating the contract. Nevertheless, you should make the final decisions and approve everything. Therefore you still need to be aware of the main legal implications.

If you do not have an agent, should you get one? You may not have previously approached any, or perhaps you found that they were 'not taking on any new authors at present'. You are unlikely to meet reluctance when a publisher is already keen to sign up your book. (Unfortunately agents rarely take on academic or educational writers, or poets.)

The main advantage of having a good agent is the benefit of his/her experience, negotiating skills and knowledge of publishing practice.

The main disadvantage is the agent's 'cut', which means less financial reward for you.

Making the decision

Although many successful authors are unrepresented, it is probably advisable for new authors to be agented. A good agent can help you structure your writing career from the outset.

The agent must be suitable for your type of writing and for you as an individual. Get recommendations from other writers or any professional bodies you join. (See addresses at the back of this book.) Research also in *The Writers' and Artists' Yearbook* or *The Writer's Handbook*. Also look at agents' websites.

You may have to approach a number of agencies before you find one willing to take you on that is suitable for you. A face-to-face meeting before you agree to accept any agent is advisable. At the meeting you can discuss the terms of the relationship and make sure that the agent is on the ball. A good agent should have:

- an understanding of copyright law, contract and royalty statements;

- a talent for selling work to publishers and getting commissions for writers;

- enthusiasm for your work and commitment to your success as a writer.

Try to get an idea of the current client list and recent successes to gauge the agent's calibre. Make it clear that you will expect to be kept reasonably informed of progress and might wish to discuss your overall career from time to time.

The agency contract

Most agents will offer you their standard terms. Sometimes this will be in a document for signature, perhaps based on the model form letter of agreement produced by the Association of Author's Agents. (If the agent is a member of this, it can be a good sign, as he/she will be subject to a code of practice.) If not, make sure you get a letter at least, setting out what has been agreed. Some points to check are:

The agent's commission

This is usually around 10 to 15% of any British royalties you receive (though many agents are now at the top end of that band). Around 15 to 20% may be reasonable on US rights or other foreign sales and multimedia sales.

Warning – if you are asked for any form of fee up-front, be very wary of using that agent. Reputable agencies rarely ask for this and do not charge 'reading fees'. (Some novice writers have lost money as the victims of various scams by sham agencies, who entice money from them.)

Termination

Resist any stipulation that suggests that the agency arrangement is 'irrevocable'. An express termination clause, stating how the agency can end, is useful. This could include provision for termination upon either party serving written notice, say three months. This will usually be without prejudice to subsisting arrangements. If the agent has, for example, sold a particular book to a publisher then he/she should continue to get the income specified in respect of that book.

Agent's authority

Be clear about the scope you wish to give to the agent (particularly regarding rights to be retained). State whether he/she is to handle all your work or just part of it; for example, novels but not plays.

Stipulate that the agent can negotiate but has no authority to enter a contract for you. (Other types of agent can do this in law.) Be careful not to 'hold-out' (represent) to a publisher that your agent has such power. Otherwise the agent can be seen as having 'ostensible' or apparent authority, and may bind you to something agreed without your consent.

◆ Your contract will normally be with the agency, not a particular person who works there.

Many agencies are limited companies, some are partnerships and some carry on business as sole traders, e.g. one man/woman businesses.

SOURCING OTHER HELP

All writers should consider **joining a professional body** such as the Society of Authors and/or the Writers' Guild. There is strength in numbers and these organisations give worthwhile services to members, not to mention bringing about valuable improvements within the sector for the good of writers as a whole.

If you are negotiating a publishing contract, they can assist you. The Society of Authors, for example, offers a **contract vetting service** to its members. It will normally consider the contract and issue an advice/letter to you about points to take up with your publisher, based on its expertise and knowledge of current publishing practice. Other membership benefits include (amongst others):

- a quarterly journal;

- networking opportunities;

- free ALCS membership (see also Chapter 5);

- advice on professional issues/problems;

- certain bookshop discounts;

- preferential rates on some items (for example, tax insurance).

Talks and events relevant to writers are held by the Society, many in London but also several further afield through the **Authors North sub-group**. The current annual membership fee is around £85.

The Writers' Guild offers similar benefits and is traditionally more the preserve of dramatists and script writers. However, both bodies cater for all types of writers and both are very useful. Addresses/websites are given at the back of this book.

You can consult your professional body on technical issues whether you have an agent or not. Regarding contract matters, writers without an agent probably benefit most from them, but even established and agented writers sometimes value a second opinion or guidance on particular points.

You may also consider instructing a solicitor to act for you on entering a publishing contract. Solicitors can be expensive, but sometimes they can obtain terms for you that ultimately compensate in the long run. It is a good idea to obtain a recommendation for a particular lawyer from another writer.

GETTING INVOLVED IN THE NEGOTIATING PROCESS

Whether or not you have an agent, it is useful to have an understanding of the negotiating practice. There are no rules as such and each situation will be individual. However, preparing yourself by considering relevant issues in advance can place you in a better position to reach a good deal. The following is a non-exhaustive list of questions to address.

- What is the status of and how established is the publisher you are dealing with?

- What are the publisher's strengths and weaknesses?

- How strong do you feel your own negotiating position to be?

- Is the person with whom you are negotiating a senior executive able to make a final decision?

- What are your main aims and what essentially do you want (for example, do you have any 'deal-breaker' requirements on which you will not give way)?

- Is the publisher trying to rush you into signing? (If so, be wary and resist this.)

Actual negotiations are likely to take place at a face to face meeting, though some may also be conducted over the telephone or via correspondence or email. Keep in mind that:

- the starting point for your next contract is likely to be your first contract, so it may pay to give negotiations for this your best shot;

- a publisher's initial offer is unlikely to be the best and the publisher may well expect to have to increase this, for example by improving the amount of any advance;

- you should present a business-like image and keep to the point. Avoid coming across as likely to be a time-waster or 'high-maintenance' author;

- you need to be realistic and reasonable. Hold out for what is really important to you but be willing to compromise on some matters.

This is, hopefully, the beginning of a fruitful relationship for you with the publisher. The contract will form the basis of this, so the negotiations for it and how you conduct yourself in them will have long-term importance.

INSISTING ON THE ESSENTIALS

Turning to the actual documentation

You will probably find that publishers offer you their standard contract. You can still negotiate for reasonable improvements on some of this.

A few (including some large houses such as Faber and Headline) have adopted a form of the **Minimum Terms Agreement** (MTA) initiated by the Society of Authors and the Writers' Guild. This should be offered to you if you are a member of either.

All contracts depend on individual circumstances. For example, contracts for academic and technical books can be very different. General points are discussed below, but may not apply in every case. Certain sample clauses will then be looked at in more depth.

What should you try to ensure is included?
Some of the main provisions to aim for (many already in the MTA) are:

- description of the work including title, length, whether hardback/paperback, illustrations (if any);

- initial print run intended;

- an advance (see later);

- royalties (see later);

- anticipated retail price;

- provision for made-up accounts preferably every six months and prompt payment of royalties, with information as per the **Model Royalty Statement** (agreed between the Society of Authors and the Publishers Association);

- provision for you to consent to/be informed of any sub-licences (see later);

- rights to be granted to the publisher or reserved by you (see later);

- no provision for a print on demand (POD) version without your prior consent or, if not, with safeguards such as no POD rights to be ever sub-licensed;

- a realistic delivery date for the typescript (usually emailed or on disk, with hard copy), avoiding 'time to be of the essence' provisions, if possible;

- the period for the publisher to state changes to the typescript;

- an undertaking and time limit for publication, e.g. within one year;

- a stipulation against change to the title without your consent;

- provision for you to be consulted on cover design and other aspects of production;

- provision for you to see proofs and make corrections;

- provision for a publisher's contribution to any expenses, such as illustration quotation fees and indexing or at least that such fees shall be deducted from royalties (to avoid your having to pay these upfront);

- provision for you to inspect the publisher's accounts relating to your work;

- a review date for the contract; for example, every ten years;

- provision for about six to 12 (or more) free copies and a discount on purchasing extra copies;

- an assertion of your paternity right (see Chapter 2);

- provision for a further assertion, copyright notice and prominent credit to you on the title page and cover (with similar provision to be in any sub-licence);

- a termination clause (see Chapter 7);

- a confidentiality clause (see Chapter 3);

- provision against the publisher assigning rights under the contract without your consent.

Advances

Aim for any advance to be non-returnable and paid on signature (often it will be on publication). It is likely to be based on a proportion of expected earnings from the first print run (probably around two thirds). Advances vary. You may not even get one, especially as a new writer, or it may be a nominal amount only.

Royalties

Following the demise of the Net Book Agreement in 1995, royalties have been generally on the basis of the book's recommended retail price (RRP). Often they range from 10% to 15% depending on such factors as the number of copies involved, and whether hardback or paperback, with smaller rates generally paid on children's books and special provisions for discounted sales. Unfortunately, heavy **discounting** has grown in recent times. Some agents are accepting a smaller royalty, such as four fifths of the normal royalty, where there is over a 50% discount to a bookseller. However, they may then restrict the amount of sales that can be discounted in any year. The publisher may require a net receipt basis. You should then aim for a higher rate of 15% or over. It is likely that in time receipts-based royalties will erode the RRP system, but there is suspicion that this will be to many authors' disadvantage.

Rights in your work

Some important factors, together with subsidiary rights and their usual publishing terminology, are discussed below, with points on how you might negotiate on these.

Copyright in your work

Many authors used to assign this outright, with the publisher buying full rights for the copyright period. Some publishers still require this, especially with new writers. **Resist** if you can, particularly if the chances are that your book may remain in print a long time. It is not advisable to agree, unless the price paid in return is very attractive. Give a **licence** allowing the publisher use of your work preferably for a specified period. This will usually be exclusive, so that you cannot license it elsewhere at the same time. The publisher is making an investment so will often require the right to publish your book in the English language worldwide for the full copyright period. With publishers becoming more global, wide territorial rights are more of a priority for them. They may agree to a shorter period for rights such as electronic rights (see later).

Sub-licensing

A publisher often grants rights to someone else out of those granted by you. This is important to a publisher's profitability.

Ideally you will want sub-licences to be subject to your consent. The phrase 'such consent not to be unreasonably withheld' often appears in any legal document where consent is mentioned. It effectively means that if you refuse, the publisher could try to obtain a declaration that this is unreasonable and get the court's 'go-ahead' instead.

A more modest goal may be to obtain an agreement that you be consulted before completion of any sub-licence.

Specify your income share. Aim for around a 60:40 split in your favour as regards royalties from sub-licensed paperback editions.

US rights

These are important and often retained by authors/their agents to sell elsewhere. If not, the contract should state the income you will receive from these, which may depend on the exact arrangements with any US publisher. You should stipulate that you approve any offers received or are at least consulted about these.

Television, radio, film and dramatic rights

These are also often retained by authors/their agents in hope of arranging a profitable deal elsewhere. If granted to a publisher, make sure you receive a high percentage (over 80%). Media contracts represent a complex area, making specialist help even more advisable, such as from a media lawyer. Some agencies specialise in media rights or have a media division, often with an 'in-house' lawyer.

Bookclub rights

Publishers often want to sell to book clubs for an all-in price, in which case you should state that you receive a royalty of 10% or above on these sales. If there is also provision for the publisher to sell copies to a book club with royalties paid on top, then press for at least 50% of these.

Special sales

Occasionally a publisher might agree to participate in a special offer, for example when a magazine gives a free novel with an issue. Usually the magazine buys the books cheaply, which could mean you receive a **reduced royalty**. It may well be you decide to go along with this, because good publicity will be generated and pick up readers who will buy your next novel. However, it is best if you can agree in advance that all such deals will be subject to your approval.

Reprographic rights

These mainly relate to photocopying (see Chapter 3). They are usually specified to be handled for the author by ALCS (see Chapters 2 and 5) and for the publisher by the Publishers Licensing Society. The contract should include provision for ALCS to handle appropriate rights (including rental rights) for you.

Public Lending Right

This was a hard-fought right, which enables authors to receive payment from library borrowing. Income depends on how often your books are taken out, but is not often very substantial. To register, obtain a form from the Public Lending Right Office. (See addresses at the back of this book.) You can also register online.

Unfortunately PLR has come under threat of reduction in recent times.

Electronic rights

This is an ever-changing area, with increasing complexity. Much will depend upon your own circumstances and the electronic opportunities applying to your particular work.

However, do not overlook this area, as such rights are becoming increasingly valuable, especially for specialist non-fiction. In 2006 came the first novel available only as a digital download. The popularity of such as **Netlibrary** is growing and audiobooks are now much in demand, especially for use with iPods. Unfortunately recent results of the ALCS Digital Survey indicated that many writers did not have relevant clauses in their contracts or were unaware whether they did or not.

When you are entering a contract for your book to be published in traditional form, it will normally be best to **retain** electronic rights, together with mechanical rights such as to publish in an audio form. This is especially so if you are retaining rights such as US rights (as online publication, which is effectively worldwide, could prevent a later deal on these). However, many publishers will want 'e-book' and audiobook rights. Try to agree **royalties**, either

◆ at the outset, if the publisher has immediate intention to publish in electronic form; *or*

◆ with provision to agree the amount, when electronic publishing becomes a real prospect.

There is a strong argument for much larger royalties than on conventional publishing, because the publisher may have less cost (for example, warehousing) involved. Try to stipulate also that the retail price remains at least 80% of the traditional version.

It is a good idea to provide for a **review** of royalties, such as after two years, because of the changing market and technological developments in this area. You could also state that the rights should **revert** to you within a certain period, if not used by the publisher.

In any contract granting such rights (for example, if your book is to be published on CD-Rom) you should still bear in mind the points applying to an ordinary book contract. An exclusive licence may often be the most suitable way to deal with electronic rights. You might perhaps grant this for only a few years, in view of how quickly the background can change. Other issues relating to traditional publishing will be relevant, especially an undertaking by the publisher to publish within a certain time, sub-licences (upon which try to aim for short periods only and more than a 50:50 split) and the inclusion of a termination clause.

Try to place a **restriction** on publishing your work in any other electronic or online form without your consent.

Because this field is so specialised and rapidly changing, the need to get advice (see earlier) on your specific circumstances applies even more, especially when entering any contract or agreeing to publication.

Bear in mind also the development of new **electronic readers**. At the time of writing, the latest of these futuristic devices is Amazon's Kindle, which has been compared to Apple's iPod and follows on the heels of Sony's successful model launched in 2006. These readers are becoming handier and look more like books. If these really take off, electronic rights will be even more important.

Other 'watch this space' areas such as Amazon and Google, involve setting up ways to **download work for payment**, which could help authors. Amazon is developing its own POD facility (see also Chapter 10). However, the Amazon Marketplace Concept has caused some consternation in some circles, as has Google's desire to own content, which could erode copyright. Such concerns have not eased in the light of Google's recent takeover of YouTube, and have raised fears over the search engine's records and privacy issues, though there may be a settlement involving Google in America that could also help some UK writers.

General online publishing

State expressly that this has to be with your consent. You would probably only allow online publishing under a short-term licence and subject to agreeing suitable remuneration. Again, many points relevant to ordinary book contracts need to be borne in mind. If your work is still unpublished, be wary of offers to publish it via the Internet. Some companies expect money from you and can represent a form of 'vanity-press'. Online publishing can sometimes make it harder to find a traditional publisher later for the work. One online publisher sets a condition that work cannot be sold to a conventional publisher for one year after it appears on the Net.

Find out how the publisher intends to advertise your work, as this will be vital to its success online.

There has been a movement, originating in the United States, towards a **creative commons licence** for material made available on the Internet. There are arguably some good intentions behind this, but be wary of giving a very wide, royalty-free, non-exclusive licence for the duration of your copyright. You may also find it difficult to prevent your work from being later changed without your consent, and you could incur liability by warranting that you have worldwide rights. That said, the number of artists using such a licence is growing. Details can be found at http://wrks.creativecommons. org.

Electrocopying

Preserving copyright in the face of technology like the Internet, where documents can often be downloaded without permission, is a challenge. A copyright notice on your work (see Chapter 2) is advisable, together with a statement that no licence to copy is to be implied just because your work is on the Internet.

Methods of preventing unauthorised copying, such as by encryption, are being developed together with electronic copyright management systems. Some writers are trying schemes for payment when copyright material is accessed on the Internet.

First serial rights

These relate primarily to periodical publications. They are the rights which you should normally give when selling stories or articles to magazines and newspapers, rather than assigning full copyright. You might also use them to grant rights for extracts of your book to be included in a newspaper or periodical before it is published.

First serial rights apply if the work has not been previously published. Depending on the country involved, they may be referred to as First British Serial Rights, First US Serial Rights, First Australian Serial Rights and so on. Some newspapers used to insist that freelances gave 'all rights', but following skilful argument to oppose this, particularly by the National Union of Journalists, this tendency is less widespread.

Second serial rights

These are similar but relate to work previously published (even if not just once but several times). They may be included in a book contract to cover, for example, where a publisher of non-fiction uses extracts in a journal. If so, you ought to specify a good royalty rate on these.

Miscellaneous rights

Other rights (many being potentially very valuable) may be covered by (or reserved in) the contract, sometimes with controlling provisions in your favour. Examples are:

- condensation rights for books/magazines;

- strip cartoon rights;

- one-shot periodical;

- merchandising;

- large print rights;

- anthology and quotation rights;

- translation rights.

The contract should specify the percentage you will receive on any you grant, ideally not less than 50%, with more on some – particularly merchandising and translation. Clauses on the licensing and sale of characters are becoming more common, particularly in America, though the legal foundation and status of such elements and purported rights is not yet fully certain.

Provisions relating to POD are now very important (see Chapter 7). Make clear that no POD rights will be sub-licensed without your approval (and preferably, that there will be no POD version at all without your consent).

Catch-all

A 'safety-net' clause should be included stating that all rights not specifically granted to the publisher are reserved by you.

CHECKING THE SMALL PRINT

How successful you are at negotiating amendments to a publisher's standard contract depends upon your own/your agent's bargaining power and ability. You may find that the contrast contains nothing too disadvantageous – but do **read it**. The case of *Interfoto* v. *Stilletto* (1988) indicated that any very unusual or onerous clause should be specifically drawn to the attention – but you should always first check through anything you sign.

Figure 4 lists some sample clauses which you are likely to encounter, divided into those which are probably acceptable and those which you may wish to resist. (The circumstances of each individual's case may, however, make the boundaries less distinct.)

What's in a word?

There can be no 'one size fits all', when it comes to the wording of a contract. That is why you should **get advice on your specific circumstances** (see earlier). However, sample clauses relevant to important issues are set out below to illustrate the type and style of drafting that can be involved (sometimes with fairly austere and old-fashioned language, despite the move towards plain English in recent times).

Note that **parts of these clauses are purposely badly drawn up**, in order to show and comment upon the **amendments that could be required**.

Copyright

'IN CONSIDERATION of the payment to the Author herein referred to, the Author hereby grants to the Publisher exclusive license to print publish sell and distribute the Work throughout the world, together with any adaptation, abridgement or substantial part thereof and for the avoidance of doubt including:

REASONABLE	UNREASONABLE
Warranty by you that the work is original, unpublished, does not infringe copyright, is not libellous and, for non-fiction, is accurate, (plus an indemnity if it proves otherwise).	An 'acceptance clause' making publication subject to acceptance of the typescript. This can mean the contract just shows intent to consider publication. (Difficult clause to negotiate upon.)
Sometimes, right of first refusal over your next book. (Usually more advisable than giving an option to the publisher.)	A contribution from you towards production costs. (This may indicate you are dealing with so-called 'vanity-press'.)
The publisher is to have control over production.	You are not even to be consulted on production.
With non-fiction particularly, your promise not to produce a competing work while this is in print.	A prohibition against you producing any similar work, so precluding, for example, short articles.
Publisher's right to 'remainder' (dispose of surplus copies very cheaply, usually to a remainder merchant).	No minimum time (e.g. 12 months) before remaindering, no royalties on remainders or option for you to purchase surplus instead.

Fig. 4. Table of sample contract clauses.

a) in hardback and paperback; and

b) as an electronic book

for the full legal term of copyright together with the right to license others to do any of the aforesaid.'

This clause amounts to a wide licence, which includes **e-book rights**. The amount of payment should therefore reflect this, or otherwise limitations could be negotiated, such as exclusion of e-book rights and provision for the author's consent to sub-licences.

Delivery of typescript

'The Author shall deliver to the Publisher not later than (*date to be inserted*) a completed typescript acceptable to the Publisher. The Publisher shall notify the Author of acceptance or rejection within one month of receipt.'

Anything like the above clause that seeks to make publication subject to acceptance or approval by the publisher **should be resisted**. Instead, a description of certain agreed criteria that the finished typescript will fulfil may be reasonable.

Several years ago, a well-publicised case involving actress-writer Joan Collins showed how difficult it is for any publisher to escape contractual obligations, unless there is a clearly expressed 'acceptance clause'. A writer therefore should never accept one in the contract.

Copyright attribution and moral rights

'The Publisher agrees that the Author's name (or any alias or pen name previously agreed in writing between the Publisher and the Author) shall appear in its customary form with due prominence on the title page and on the binding and jacket of every copy of the Work published by the Publisher, and that the Publisher shall make it a condition of contract that a similar agreement is made in respect of any licensed editions of the Work.

The Author hereby asserts to the Publisher his/her moral right to be identified as Author of the Work pursuant to sections 77 and 78 of the Copyright Designs and Patents Act 1988. The Publisher hereby undertakes to print a notice in accordance with this in every copy of the Work published by the Publisher and to require the Publisher's licensees to include such a notice on any edition of the Work published by such licensees.'

Provisions of this type usually cause no controversy but it is important to assert the right to be identified as the author (see Chapter 2).

Complete agreement

'This Agreement represents the entire and complete understanding reached by the Author and the Publisher and supersedes any earlier agreement or understanding, whether oral or in writing, in relation to the Work and the subject matter of this Agreement.'

The effect of this is that no contractual provisions are to apply other than those set out in the written contract. If you are wishing to rely on such as verbal assurances from the publisher, you should make sure that these are written into the contract or you will find it very difficult to claim than they were part of the agreement reached.

(Note that the actual contractual document may go by various names, for example 'contract', 'agreement', or even 'memorandum of agreement'. What matters is that it amounts to being binding, as most signed documents in these circumstances will do. See also Chapter 5 for the basic elements required for an agreement to be binding.)

Copyright infringement

'If the Publisher deems that the copyright in the Work has been infringed, the Publisher shall be entitled to take such steps as it sees as necessary to remedy this matter, including proceedings to be at the Publisher's expense. Subject to the Publisher giving an indemnity to the Author against liability for costs and expense, the Author shall be joined as party to any such proceedings if required by the Publisher. Any damages or profits recovered in relation to such infringement shall be shared equally between the Publisher and the Author, after deduction of costs and expenses incurred.'

This is a standard provision often inserted by publishers. It allows them to pursue anyone who infringes your copyright, so is to both your and the Publisher's advantage.

Accounting periods

'The Publisher shall render statements of sales to the Author each month following publication and undertakes to pay all royalties due each month promptly and without undue delay with time to be of the essence.'

Dream on! Unfortunately publishers will rarely give a promise in these terms. However, an undertaking to account should be included, with the details pinned down as much as you can.

CASE STUDIES

Liz goes online

Liz has written a novella, an extract of which she places on her own website. This attracts the attention of an online publisher, who contacts her through the website asking to see the full text. Liz emails this and the publisher offers to publish this online.

Liz is tempted at first but the contract terms emailed to her are vague as to the remuneration she will receive. There is also a reference to the author 'contributing to promotional and related costs'. Liz is concerned that this could be a veiled form of vanity publishing. Furthermore she has plans to revise the novella into a full-length novel, which she can then try to place with an agent. In the end, she declines the online offer.

Bill is 'signed-up'

After many rejections, Bill has finally found a publisher for the biography. It is a fairly specialised, small firm. Bill is offered its standard contract.

There is no advance but the royalties seem reasonable. Bill's concern is the cost of photographs and illustrations for the book. He finds it difficult to fund these 'up front'.

As Bill is a new author, the lack of advance may not necessarily be unreasonable. He must ensure he is not being asked for any subsidy himself (and is not involved with 'vanity-press'). Bill should bear in mind the contract points listed in this chapter and also consider obtaining advice. He could, for example, join the Society of Authors and have the contract vetted by them. He should explain his financial situation to the publisher and seek to negotiate a 'picture budget' to cover the costs of photographs and illustrations or at least obtain a contribution.

Daniel gets agented

After his problems with the TV company, Daniel decides that having an agent may strengthen his position. He has joined the Writers' Guild (traditionally more focused on drama, TV and radio and having amalgamated with the Theatre Writers' Union). From them, he receives recommendations as to suitable agents who specialise in television work and who are members of the Association of Authors' Agents or the Personal Managers' Association, so have a code of professional behaviour. He finds an agent who will take him on now that he is becoming fairly well-known, and is able to advise him on particular provisions required in any contract, such as repeat fees.

Daniel should ensure the agency contract is in writing. He should also consider obtaining legal advice before he commits himself. He should clarify whether the agency relates to all his work or just his television work. The agent then knows the basis of any commission. This aspect can cause friction if not made clear at the outset.

SUMMARY

◆ If you obtain an agent, ensure the agency arrangements are noted in writing.

◆ With book publishers, a formal contract should be drawn up. In particular clarify royalties, the rights you are granting and the rights you retain.

◆ Seek advice/representation on specific terms. Possible sources include your agent, your solicitor, the Society of Authors and the Writers' Guild.

◆ Make sure you understand the terms before you sign. If necessary, ask for clarification and negotiate. Be polite, to the point and professional in such dealings.

POINTS TO CONSIDER

1. Set out, in order of priority, the realistic terms you would aim to agree in a book contract.

2. Consider which contract clauses you would strongly resist.

3. What alternative compromises might you put forward to a publisher?

7

Getting Out of a Contract

I writ them a bill with mine own blood: the date is expired, this is the time, and he will fetch me.

(*Doctor Faustus*, Scene XIX, Christopher Marlowe)

WHAT IF IT ALL GOES WRONG?

Getting into a contract is easier than getting out of one. That is why it is important to ensure that the terms you agree to are ones which you can live with in the long term (see Chapters 5 and 6). That said, not even the crystal ball of a writer's imagination can foresee everything. An arrangement which suited you earlier may prove a millstone later. Therefore in this chapter you will look at potential 'get-outs'.

WHEN IS A CONTRACT NOT A CONTRACT?

The first possibility is to deny that a contract ever existed.

Certain **vitiating factors** can mean there never was true agreement. The contract is *void ab initio* (invalid from the beginning) or *voidable* (so that a party can elect to treat it as invalid).

Mistake

This is not a mistake in the ordinary sense. You might feel that a contract has been a big mistake. Perhaps it was not as profitable as you hoped. The law sees this as a mere mistake **as to quality**. To invalidate a contract the mistake has to be **fundamental**: for example, if you contracted to write a guidebook on Richmond, meaning the town in North Yorkshire, but the publisher intended Richmond-on-Thames.

Duress and undue influence

These apply where threat or coercion is used to make you enter a contract. The publisher may not literally hold a gun to your head, but what about metaphorically?

The modern concept of **economic duress** could be relevant. For this, there has to be more than just commercial pressure. Suppose, however, you complete a commissioned book but the publisher will only proceed if you agree to less royalties. You point to the original terms, but the publisher gambles on your desperate need for funds. You reluctantly agree to the new terms. In some circumstances it might be possible to argue later that the second agreement be overturned on grounds of economic duress (linked with lack of consideration – see Chapter 5).

Misrepresentation

This is where a person makes an **untrue statement of fact** to **induce** another to enter a contract.

This might apply, for example, where in certain circumstances a publisher grossly exaggerates to you the amount you will receive or the extent of promotion for your book. If you prove misrepresentation, you may be entitled to **rescind** (undo) the contract and/or obtain damages.

HOW CAN I END MY CONTRACT?

The law recognises certain ways in which a contract may end. Some are amicable, some more hostile.

By agreement

No problem here. You and your agent or publisher (depending on the particular contract involved) agree to part company. This agreement is a new contract, superseding and releasing you both from the previous one.

By performance

Again no problem. You have fulfilled your part and your agent/ publisher has fulfilled theirs. The contract expires because its purpose is satisfied; for example a one-off commission for a set fee.

By frustration (or impossibility)

This occurs when **a contract is prevented** from being carried out, **not through the fault of either party**, but by an intervening event.

The event must be drastic enough to fundamentally change the circumstances **and** be something not contemplated at the time of the contract.

Sometimes a contract will include a *force majeure* clause giving a long list of intervening eventualities such as war or strike action. A short example, which aims to protect a writer, is:

> 'The Author shall not be liable for any failure in the performance of any of his/her obligations under this contract caused by factors outside his/her control.'

A commission to write a book is in effect a contract for personal service. You cannot subcontract to another author (unless you are a celebrity and ghost-writing is envisaged). If you cannot perform your obligations, because of, say, a **serious** accident, you could argue that the contract has been frustrated through personal incapacity, not that you are in breach because you cannot complete the work. This is supported by a 1960s case which held that, when the drummer of 'The Barron Knights' pop group was too ill to perform, the contract was frustrated.

Example

You are commissioned to write a travelogue relating to a proposed visit to an African region. You find you cannot get there because of an outbreak of hostilities in the region. You might put forward a claim that the contract had therefore been frustrated. You could find you must return any advance, but may be allowed to deduct expenses properly incurred.

By breach

If you or the agent/publisher fail to carry out relevant obligations, on the face of it this is **breach of contract**. The innocent party can claim damages from the other (see later). (Depending on the circumstances, the publisher may also be in breach of the Publishers' Association Code of Practice.)

It matters whether the obligation breached amounts to an important term of the contract or not. If so, this is legally classified as a **condition** rather than a **warranty** (a subsidiary provision – not to be confused with the same word meaning a type of guarantee). If there is a breach of condition, then the contract can be regarded as **discharged**. The innocent party can claim damages **and** treat the contract as being at an end.

Terms likely to amount to conditions in a book contract are such as:

- on the publisher's part, the promise to publish and to pay royalties;

- on your part, the promise to complete a typescript and to correct proofs.

Provisions such as that the publisher will consult you on production or that you are entitled to free copies are more likely to be considered warranties, leading to just a claim for compensation.

USING A TERMINATION CLAUSE

A termination clause in your contract could prove useful if things turn sour. It may also help you establish that rights in your work have reverted to you.

It can cover **automatic** termination on certain events (like the publisher going into liquidation). It may allow you to **give notice** to bring the contract to an end in particular circumstances. Keep a copy of any letter giving notice and send it by recorded delivery.

Figure 5 contains a sample termination clause to give you an idea of the events which might be covered in a contract with a publisher. Note that termination is stated at point 3 not to wipe out existing claims under the contract, for example, for outstanding royalties.

The exact clause suitable for your own contract depends on your circumstances and specific advice should be sought (see Chapter 6). Additional points may be covered, such as a definition of 'out of print', particularly in the light of new 'print on demand'

1. This contract shall terminate automatically if the Publisher convenes a meeting of its creditors or suffers a petition to be presented or other action to be taken with a view to its liquidation (other than for the purposes of and followed by amalgamation or reconstruction) or an administration order is made in relation to it or a receiver appointed over any of its property.

2. The Author may by 30 days' written notice terminate this contract or suspend his/her performance of all or any of his/her obligations under it immediately and without liability for damages or other remedy if:

   a. the Publisher fails to comply with any of its obligations under this contract after one-month's written notice from the Author requesting it to do so; or

   b. all editions of the Work are out of print (other than any print on demand or electronic editions) and the Publisher does not confirm its intention to reprint or reissue such Work (other than as in POD versions or electronic editions) within 30 days of written request to do so by the author; or

   c. less than 30 copies of the hardback edition or less than 100 copies of the paperback edition of the Work are sold throughout any two consecutive royalty accounting periods.

3. Upon termination, all rights in the Work shall revert to the Author, but termination shall be without prejudice to any sub-licences properly granted by the Publisher (but the Publisher undertakes not to grant such sub-licenses after service of notice of termination) or any claim or right of action already accrued to either party in respect of any breach of this contract by the other party or claim for monies due to the Author.

Fig. 5. Sample termination clause.

technology. Safeguards like insertion of a sales threshold and/or option to terminate upon a switch to print-on-demand, are advisable. If there is a clause allowing the publisher to terminate, avoid loose-wording and wide 'get-outs', such as one week's notice without any reason.

Print on demand (POD)

This is a digital process that allows books to be **printed as required** in small amounts or even as one-off items. Quality has recently improved and many publishers may use this process, cutting costs such as warehousing. In many ways, it is a welcome development.

However, advances in this technology have brought some headaches when it comes to contracts. If your book stays available through this, how can it ever be said to be out of print? And if it is never out of print, **how can you ever get your rights back**, if you want them? This is where **the right wording in your contract is vital**. Take advice on your specific circumstances (see Chapter 6).

Under the MTA (see Chapter 6), the publisher should notify you if your book becomes out of print. Often publishers forget to do so, but if you no longer receive any royalty statements, this may be the case and you should check the position with the publisher.

The sample termination clause in Figure 5 sets out to exclude POD and electronic editions for the purposes of the 'out of print' provision at clause 2(b). Otherwise this provision could never apply, if POD remained available for the work. If the book is never technically out of print, it could languish with a publisher who may over-price it and do little to promote it or satisfy orders promptly. Clause 2(c) gives a **threshold of minimum sales**. If you have the right to terminate, in the event that orders fall very low, you can at least then see if a different, more proactive publisher might take your book instead. You might also **consider self-publishing** (see Chapter 10).

GETTING REDRESS

Suppose the agent/publisher fails to fulfil contractual obligations? Probably the most frequent example is a publisher's refusal to publish your book – the publisher 'cancels the contract'. (This is colloquial, not legal terminology.) If this is not caused by your fault and you have fulfilled your side of the contract, then assuming the publisher has no relevant 'get out' like an acceptance clause (see Chapter 6), what can you do?

Conciliation

Try to talk the situation through. Establish what the problem is. If a publisher has reservations about your typescript, for example, discuss possible changes. If the situation cannot be salvaged, discuss compensation. Generally, a negotiated out-of-court settlement is better for both parties. It avoids risk of losing, cost of litigation and unwelcome publicity. You many need to seek legal advice at this stage.

If a compromise cannot be reached, you may have to consider your legal remedies. Even if the publisher makes an offer of settlement, you need to have some idea of the legal options to assess whether to accept, or to take your chances in court (see also Chapter 8).

Specific performance

This is an order compelling someone to perform their part of the contract. It is given at the court's discretion and not very often. Because it is an equitable remedy, certain maxims (principles) apply, including that you must have 'clean hands'. In other words, you must not be at fault in any way in the matter to have any chance of obtaining this order.

Damages

The courts award damages for breach of contract on the basis that you should be put in the same position **as if the contract was properly carried out**. This means that you should, in theory, receive compensation equal to the amount you would have received if the publisher had kept to the contract. This could include any unpaid advance and the royalties you were likely to earn, at least on the first print run.

You must, however, bear in mind that you are under a **duty to mitigate**. This means you have to do whatever you reasonably can to lessen your loss. You may have to show that you tried to find another publisher, or even improvise where appropriate, by adapting a non-fiction work into articles. Any damages will be reduced accordingly.

One way to avoid a duty to mitigate can be to claim on a *quantum meruit* basis. This lawyer's Latin means basically that a fair sum should be paid for work done up to a certain point. You may be able to claim this where you are ready to fulfil your contractual obligations but the publisher in effect prevents you from doing so.

Example

In one case, an author was commissioned to write a volume on costume and ancient armour for a set fee payable on publication. He wrote part and would have completed the work, except for discovering that the publisher had ceased to publish the periodical for which the volume was required. The court awarded the writer half the set fee for work done so far. There was no onus on him to seek publication elsewhere.

CASE STUDIES

Liz fails the deadline

Liz has a commission in writing for a magazine feature on skiing in Scotland, where she is to visit an appropriate resort. This is required for a January issue by a strict copy date. Whilst practising on a local dry-ski slope, she suffers serious injury and is unable to travel or work at that time.

Liz must inform the magazine as soon as possible. Her notification that she will be unable to deliver the feature for the deadline could be seen as **an anticipatory breach of contract** (a breach of obligation set to happen). She can argue instead that the contract has been frustrated because the intervening accident made it impossible for her to carry it out. If the magazine disputes this, she may need a doctor's statement. In any event, the magazine would be under a duty to mitigate its loss. It should be able to make alternative arrangements, given the current supply of freelance writers.

Bill the 'terminator'

Bill's publishers are dragging their heels even though it is nearly the centenary of the biographee's death. The contract, dated over a year previously, states that publication is to be within eighteen months. The publishers assured Bill verbally when he signed, that they were keen to publish within six months. Bill is now sceptical of the publishers ever bringing the book out. There is a termination clause in the contract.

Bill should take a firm stance. He should stress the eighteen-month period in the contract. He could even suggest misrepresentation as regards the verbal promises regarding six months. Bill can also point to the termination clause. Assuming it allows him to serve notice on breach of obligation by the publisher, he should make clear that he will not hesitate to do so – and claim damages. This may force the issue, but at least he will find out the publisher's true intention. His threats may make them think hard before 'cancelling'. Bill should stress the marketing opportunities which the centenary event could bring, to rekindle the publisher's enthusiasm.

Daniel ends a beautiful friendship

Daniel finds that he has a personality clash with his new agent. He has since had recommended another agent, who has more expertise in his particular field.

Daniel should discuss the situation with the first agent and point out that he feels that the relationship is not working. He should not previously have agreed to any attempt to make the agency irrevocable (see Chapter 5). If there is a termination clause in the agency contract, he should give written notice under this. The usual basis is that the agent will continue to receive any income due on deals he has previously arranged as Daniel's agent. It should be clarified whether the agent is to continue to sell rights in earlier work or whether all unsold work is to pass to the new agent.

SUMMARY

If you wish to end your contract:

◆ Consider whether any special factors could make it invalid, such as misrepresentation.

◆ Can it be ended by agreement, or alternatively has any unforeseen event intervened to frustrate the contract?

◆ If you have a termination clause in the contract, use it where applicable. Serve any notice by recorded delivery.

◆ Check whether the other party has failed to observe a condition so that you can treat the contract as discharged – and claim damages.

◆ Take legal advice where necessary and try to negotiate a solution where appropriate.

◆ If this is not possible, the legal remedy you are most likely to obtain for breach is damages.

◆ Such damages should be based on the amount you would have earned under the contract, subject to your duty to mitigate.

POINTS TO CONSIDER

1. Which of the following could amount to misrepresentation:

   – a publisher, on picking up the signed contract which you have just placed on his desk, says, 'You won't regret this. You'll make a packet.'

   – a publisher, on handing to you the contract for signature, says 'No doubt you'll be giving up the day job. Thirty thousand at least for you on the first print run.'

2. Taking the usual terms of a book contract (see Chapter 6), consider which may be important enough to be conditions, and which are likely to be only warranties.

3. Suppose a publisher 'cancels' a contract with you when you are a third of the way through the book and have incurred expenses of £100 in research. The advance agreed was £500. You estimate you would have received royalties of about £8,000. Think about the level of compensation for which you would press.

8

Getting Paid

No man but a blockhead ever wrote, except for money.
(Samuel Johnson, *Life of Johnson*, (J. Boswell) Vol. III.)

TAKING 'PERSUASIVE' MEASURES

You might feel that having sold your writing, you have done the hard part. Getting the money in can be even harder.

Many professional writers have 'cashflow difficulties' and are owed money by at least one publisher at any given time.

What can you do about it?

You must appreciate that as a mere writer, some publishers regard you as a low priority when it comes to payment. The same can apply to illustrators, photographers and models.

Publishers often have a different attitude towards their commercial suppliers. Therefore it can help to project the right image – professional and businesslike, not disorganised and eccentric.

Your 'credit control' steps

Below are some suggestions relating to articles, stories and other freelance items.

Before payment is due:

♦ Ensure any commission or acceptance is in writing (see Chapter 5).

◆ Send an invoice.

After payment is due:

◆ Send a reminder.

◆ Send another reminder seven days later.

◆ Telephone the accounts department.

◆ Telephone the editor.

◆ Send a letter before action setting out your claim and warning of proceedings.

Always keep a copy of everything.

The invoice

This should preferably be on a pre-printed invoice form or letter-headed paper.

It should be headed 'INVOICE' and ideally include your name and address and those of the publisher, the name of the person who gave the commission/acceptance, a brief description of the work with any title, the sum owed, an invoice number, the present date and the due date for payment. For short stories and articles, it is often agreed that payment will be on or one month after publication.

The due date can be relevant to any interest claimed for late payment. Interest used to be only claimable if the contract expressly provided for it, or in proceedings at the rate set by the court. The Late Payment of Commercial Debts (Interest) Act 1998 allows interest to be claimed in certain other circumstances.

Send your invoice to the publisher's **accounts department**. If the organisation is too small to have one, send it to the editor.

Reminders
The contents can be similar to those of the invoice but headed 'REMINDER' or 'ACCOUNT RENDERED' or 'STATEMENT'. Set up a standard letter on your PC, if possible.

Telephoning
This can keep the pressure up. Remember the two 'P's – **politeness and persistence**.

One ploy can be to ask questions to which the answer is 'yes' or 'no'.

Example
– Did you receive my invoice?

– Do you agree this balance is due for payment?

– Will you send a cheque today?

If any dispute comes to light, such as over the exact terms previously agreed with you, try to resolve this. Exchange information and provide a copy of any documentation which clarifies the matter. (See Chapter 5.)

Putting it in writing
If unable to resolve the matter by telephone, send a letter setting out your claim and warning of proceedings. This may result in payment.

The letter should be on headed paper, be dated, refer to your invoice and when it was submitted, and state that, unless you receive payment within a specified time, you will initiate proceedings. Send it by Recorded or Special Delivery. Figure 6 gives an example. Include any other details relevant to your own claim.

Dear Sirs

Invoice number 0117 – Article on 'Healthy Food'

I refer to the above invoice in the sum of £150 which was submitted for your attention on 9 October. A copy was sent with a reminder on 9 November.

Please note that unless payment is received by me within fourteen days of the date of this letter, I will have no alternative but to commence proceedings.

Yours faithfully

Fig. 6. Letter setting out a claim ('Letter before action').

You could instruct a solicitor in this. This will entail expense but, if you limit instructions to this preparatory step, not an inordinate amount. You could ask for a quote first. (Solicitors are under pressure from the Law Society to give accurate estimates.) Sometimes an organisation will pay by return of post as soon as it receives a solicitor's letter. It looks as though you mean business.

Another alternative is to instruct a debt collecting agency. They will charge for this service.

What about book publishers?
Your contract should specify payment dates for royalties. Often it

is twice a year on set dates. Diarise these. If payment does not arrive around this time, get in touch with any agent who negotiated the contract or telephone the publisher's accounts department. Again politeness and persistence pays.

DECIDING TO SUE

You must take a commercial decision whether to sue or accept this unprofessional treatment for the sake of future goodwill.

The courts expect parties to have tried to settle matters before proceedings are begun. Make sure you have tried to resolve any dispute before you sue. Litigation should be a last resort.

As all lawyers stress, **there is no point in suing 'a man of straw'**. Look for signs whether the publication/publisher is in financial difficulties. Has it always paid promptly, but suddenly not now? Is the magazine issue coming out after its official publication date? Have many editorial staff recently left? If you suspect money trouble, it is a gamble to take further action. You could end up as another unsecured creditor, with a judgement but no assets to satisfy it.

GOING TO COURT

Since 1999 there have been changes in the court system, aiming for more **speed and economy**, not to mention **proportionality**. For many years there had been a feeling that proceedings were too lengthy, too costly and often too complex. Recommendations by Lord Woolf proposed **stream-lining the system**, leading to new **Civil Procedure Rules** with the over-riding objective of:

◆ enabling the court to deal with cases justly.

It is not possible to include every detail, but a brief overview of the system and how it can help you to bring a simple debt 'small claim' is set out here.

Which court?

High Court
You can usually only start proceedings here if the value of your claim is relatively large or in a special category.

County Court
You can use this for contract and tort claims in general, though usually up to a certain amount.

Which track?

The court now allocates cases to one of three tracks:

- **the small claims track** (usually for claims up to £5,000);

- **the fast track** (usually for larger claims, where any trial is likely to last less than a day);

- **the multi-track** (usually for large/difficult claims).

For most claims involving debts owed for freelance work, the small claims track is likely to apply. The usual time limit for bringing such a claim is six years from it arising.

How to start?

Some of the main points are set out below. If you decide to act for yourself as a **litigant in person**:

◆ Contact your local county court office for information on procedure. They can help with your specific enquiries, provide useful literature on how to bring your claim and give you the forms you will need with notes for guidance. See also www.moneyclaim.gov.uk.

◆ You as **claimant** are expected to complete a **claim form** (usually form N1), which will form a **statement of case** in your proceedings. This should include brief details of your claim, together with the amount claimed.

◆ Make sure that the person you claim against (the defendant) is correctly named. For companies, check names for free via www.companies-house.gov.uk.

◆ You must give a **statement of value**, basically being the amount claimed.

If you decide to instruct a solicitor, he or she will draft the documentation for you, but bear in mind the cost. You may also find your local Citizens' Advice Bureau is a good source of guidance in bringing your claim.

What next?

In broad terms, once you have lodged your claim at court, usually with two copies (and paid any fee required – see later), it is issued and notified to the defendant. A **response pack** is then sent, including forms for the defendant either to **admit** the claim or **defend** it. A **counterclaim** by the defendant is also a possibility. Usually the defendant must respond within fourteen days. If there is no response, you can apply for **default judgement** for the amount you claim, using the appropriate form (usually N205A or N225 in a specified debt claim).

If the defendant admits your claim, you will be notified and can request judgement (usually form N205A or N225 again). If you don't agree to the defendant's payment proposals, the court can arrange to decide this issue.

If a defence is filed, the case may be transferred to the defendant's 'home court', especially if the defendant is an individual. The court sends you and the defendant an **allocation questionnaire** (form N150). Make sure you return this by the date stipulated, with any fee required. This helps the court's **case management** and allocation of the case to the right track. The court then directs how the case will proceed, particularly regarding timescale, any steps to be taken by the parties and the setting of any trial (normally within 30 weeks).

It is less likely that a straightforward debt claim would lead to prolonged litigation. Many organisations reach for the cheque book, when proceedings commence. If there has to be a hearing, this is generally less formal for the small claims track. A **small claims hearing** will normally be before a **District Judge**. Strict rules of evidence will not apply (though most hearings will now be in public), but you will have to prove your claim. Have all your documentation and other evidence to hand. Be clear, concise and as professional as possible. There are special provisions to allow a party to give seven days' notice that they will not attend, but still have written evidence taken into account.

If you obtain judgement, but the defendant still does not pay, then you can **enforce** it through court methods, if necessary. This can involve more procedure and fees.

What might it cost?

You must bear in mind that **court fees** are entailed in proceedings, unless you are exempt, for example, if on benefits. If fees are not paid, your claim can be 'struck out'. Check with your local county court for exact figures, as these can change. They can also depend on the amount you are claiming. These can often be claimed from your defendant, if you win, together with certain out-of-pocket expenses and sometimes loss of earnings or your time up to a limit.

If you instruct a solicitor, you cannot usually recover legal costs in a case on the small claims track. In other cases you may be able to claim these, provided you win (though the court is allowed to make a different order, such as for payment of a proportion only or a stated amount). Also bear in mind that, if you lose, you may have to pay the defendant's legal costs as well.

No win, no fee

Some solicitors now take cases on a no win, no fee basis under a **conditional fee agreement**. However, there are still court fees to bear in mind and the risk of being ordered to pay the other side's costs. If you do win, the solicitor may charge more than usual.

You could ask your solicitor about legal aid, though eligibility for this has greatly narrowed in recent years.

European Small Claims Procedure

This is likely to be implemented from 2009 to give a procedure for tort or contract claims up to €2,000 arising in other EU states (except Denmark, which is subject to opt-out).

REACHING A SETTLEMENT

Most disputes never reach the courtroom. The power of your legal rights often lies more in their potential than in actual litigation. Furthermore, changes to the court system have placed emphasis on **alternative dispute resolution (ADR)**, such as mediation and upon reaching an early settlement where possible, with claimants as well as defendants able to make offers to settle.

Following a recent pilot scheme in Manchester, it is likely that courts will start to have in-house small claims mediators. Bear in mind also that sometimes disputes with publishers can be dealt with under the **Informal Dispute Settlement Scheme** run by the Publishers Association, to avoid litigation.

Where there is dispute, such as over the amount of fee agreed, and you have no conclusive evidence on your side, consider any reasonable offer put to you. Make no admission as to any fault yourself.

Generally it is better to negotiate over the telephone or face to face, rather than through correspondence. If possible, let the other side mention a figure first. If it is derisory, reject it. Otherwise, say you will get back to them, rather than make an impulsive decision. If you have incurred expense, like a court fee, ensure this is included in any amount you agree.

Any written offer will probably be headed 'without prejudice'. You would be wise to head your own correspondence with this when negotiating. It will often be implied in oral negotiations too, but it is just as well to make this clear before you start discussions. This phrase basically means that if you reject the offer, you cannot later refer to it in court to prove an admission of fault. Once you accept the offer, the correspondence loses this 'privilege'. It can then be used to prove the agreement for payment to you of the amount offered.

CASE STUDIES

Liz takes action

A magazine to which Liz has supplied stories regularly has not paid her for the last two. Both were accepted in writing with payment to be on publication, and have now been published.

Liz has already invoiced, followed by reminders and telephone chasers to the accounts department. She has sent a letter setting out her claim and warning of proceedings. The silence is still deafening. Being reasonably confident that the magazine is solvent, she now issues proceedings. The magazine sends a cheque as soon as these are served upon it, not wanting to risk a judgement being registered against it which could affect its credit rating.

Bill inspects

The biography has now been published. Sales are modest, but, partly due to local publicity, are at a reasonable level. Bill, however, has not received any royalties.

Bill checks the payment provisions in his contract and the publisher's royalty accounting periods. Payment is clearly in arrears. He contacts the publisher's accounts department to enquire whether there has been an 'oversight'. He is told they will look into it. He still receives nothing. He writes a polite letter giving notice of his intention to exercise his right to inspect the accounts so far as they relate to his book. He quotes the relevant clause in the contract containing this right, and suggests a date and time. The accounts department seems to resent this potential intrusion. A cheque and statement arrive a few days later.

Daniel settles out of court

The TV company for whom Daniel has been working wishes to bring in a new writer for the next series of the sit-com. Daniel is not too perturbed because he wants to pursue other work. His new agent has 'irons in the fire' on this. The agent had insisted that he received a written contract for the present series. Under it the TV company cannot terminate just yet.

Daniel opens negotiations for compensation through his agent. The agent recommends a media solicitor be consulted.

'Without prejudice' negotiations take place and an offer is made. Daniel is advised to reject this as insufficient. Negotiations continue. The agent and solicitor advise Daniel on a reasonable sum to accept. The TV company offer almost this amount. Daniel decides to take the 'bird in the hand'. This settlement is recorded in writing.

SUMMARY

◆ For articles, stories and similar freelance items, chase up payment through:

 – invoicing

 – reminders

 – telephone enquiries

 – a letter setting out your claim and warning of proceedings.

♦ For book publishers, diarise contractual dates and contact the publisher's accounts department as soon as you realise that payment is overdue.

♦ Try to negotiate a settlement in any dispute.

♦ Only sue if you believe your defendant to be solvent.

♦ Consider taking legal advice.

♦ Beware of the risk of costs being awarded against you if you lose, particularly with larger claims.

POINTS TO CONSIDER

1. Devise a standard invoice and reminder letter, preferably on PC, to use when need arises.

2. Contact your local county court for the appropriate leaflets and forms, so that you have these to hand.

3. Draft a standard 'letter before action'. Keep this as your template to use if necessary.

9

Sorting Out Other Problems

He that handleth a matter wisely shall find good.

(*Proverbs*, Chapter 16, verse 20)

This chapter comprises questions on common problems you may encounter, together with possible solutions.

How long can they sit on it?

You might ask this when selling articles or stories to a magazine, or when you have a manuscript with an agent or a book under consideration with a publisher.

There are few legal strictures to help you, unless you get a time expressly agreed. You can insert a limit as a device to 'encourage' editors not to keep you waiting. For example, one freelance, a former journalist with a national newspaper, inserts 'on offer for publication within two months' at the top of copy.

A good agent should give you progress reports, not fobbing-off with vague references to your work being with a publisher. The agent is acting for you after all. Find out which publishing houses have considered the manuscript and brief details of their reactions.

If a publisher takes months to respond to you, consider chasing this up diplomatically in writing or by telephone. Some publishers give warning on receipt of submissions if substantial delay is likely. If you are established on the publisher's list, press your editor when delay becomes unreasonable.

What if my material is edited without permission?

On a pragmatic basis, it is generally accepted that some editing is required to suit commercial needs. Editors usually aim to improve grammar and abbreviate when necessary. House style is relevant. Most writers welcome such assistance.

If your whole self-expression and meaning has been distorted, your moral rights (see Chapter 2) may come into play. You may be able to insist on amendment, obtain an apology or publicly disassociate yourself from the change, depending on exact circumstances.

Can I charge a 'kill-fee'?

Some freelances have made effective demands for a 'kill-fee'. One found that mention of this stopped an editor trying to back-track on a commissioned work. 'Kill-fee' is not a legal term, nor an automatic right. A few magazines pay for abortive work as their normal practice. If you have fulfilled any agreed brief and deadline for a commission, you should expect your full fee. However a 'kill-fee' may be a good compromise to preserve a relationship with an editor. You may have to show a 'kill-fee' was agreed in the contract. Be careful not to insert anything too excessive which might become a form of penalty clause, as these are technically void in law. 'Agreed damages clauses' are allowed for realistic compensation agreed in advance. Therefore, any fee stated should be a genuine estimate of your loss through cancellation. Fifty per cent of the full fee is paid by some publications and this may be a good amount for which to aim.

I have described myself in my writer's CV as a contributor to certain magazines. Do I need their permission?

Very unlikely. That said, any statement must be correct and not misleading.

A corporation has taken a large chunk from a textbook I produced and annexed copies of it to its staff manual. Is this allowed?

Almost certainly not. The *de minimus* rule and fair dealing (see Chapter 3) are unlikely to apply. Unless your publisher has some special agreement with the company you should ask him to take up this matter, possibly through the CLA (see Chapter 3).

I've at last found a publisher but he wants revisions to my work by a tight deadline. Should I take measures, like resigning my day-job, to be sure I can meet this?

The exact timescale involved may depend on whether you have agreed to a specific date in a contract and just how this has been worded and your decision must really be based on your full personal circumstances.

The decision whether to give up the day-job represents the type of dilemma that so many of us face as writers. Often it feels like 'Catch 22', in that your writing cannot take off without more time commitment, but until it does, there is very little income to be derived from it. That very inconvenient need to eat tends to intrude.

Any such major decision should be approached with caution and not taken lightly. Research commissioned by ALCS has suggested that a typical author's income is a third less than the national average wage, with most writers relying on a second job or a partner's wages to continue to write and only just over 20% of UK writers earning all their income from writing. It also indicated that earnings could be better for men than women (which seems unfair), but are presently deteriorating all round, with typical earnings for those aged 25 to 34 being around £5,000 per annum. Whilst the average income for best-selling writers might be over £80,000 per annum, a typical professional writer might earn just £4,000 per annum. An **All-Party Writers Group** has been set up to campaign for a fairer deal for writers (www.allpartywritersgroup. co.uk) but it may be some time before there is much improvement.

Bursary schemes exist, some of which are administered through the Society of Authors, but there is never enough funding to ensure that all applicants are successful. Grants and pensions from such as the Royal Literary Fund may also be available to published writers in financial difficulties (www.rlf.org.uk).

Bear in mind also that a gap in your CV may make it much harder to return to the workplace later, should you need to, and job-seekers allowance can be refused to those who give up a post voluntarily. Perhaps you could consider a compromise such as **working part time or taking a secondment**, if your employer will allow it. Of course, with writing, money is rarely the main incentive to pursue it – but then along comes that very inconvenient need to eat again!

As regards any tight deadline given by a publisher, explain your position and try to **negotiate a reasonable extension**, if necessary.

Most publishers would rather you honour a realistic agreed deadline than fail to meet an over-optimistic one.

I have got together with a friend to co-write a book. Should we leave things on an informal footing?

A written co-writers' agreement is a good idea, especially as copyright in shared work is usually owned jointly. Hopefully, your relationship will never turn sour, but recording your intentions could help prevent arguments later. Ideally the agreement should be drawn up by a solicitor or other appropriate professional adviser. The agreement should cover all relevant aspects and, in particular, include clarification of each writer's share of proceeds from the work. Consider also inserting a provision for one to buy out the other, including copyright, in case you ever do have a serious rift.

Tension can often arise if one writer feels that the other is not doing as much work. A written agreement can help to lay-down 'ground rules'. Points to consider covering in this include the following.

♦ No publishing contract is to be agreed by either of you without mutual agreement.

♦ An undertaking by you both to collaborate exclusively with one another on the work.

♦ A commitment to meet at specified regular intervals to liaise on the project and work together.

♦ On a less cheery note, what is to happen in the event of either of you dying or being incapacitated?

I have been asked to help someone write their autobiography. What issues could arise?

Many of the points in the answer to the preceding question are also relevant here.

If you are being asked in effect to **ghostwrite** the autobiography of, for example, a celebrity or other famous person, there may already be a publisher lined up. See Chapters 5 and 6 regarding contracts and seek help from an agent or other sources on the specifics involved in your situation.

If the person is not well known and no publisher has yet been found, a written agreement between you is still important and the same caveat about seeking help on specifics can still apply. You may wish to stipulate that you be **paid whether or not the work is eventually published**. Ask for the person's permission for you to have **access to private papers, letters, journals etc.**, with their **consent given to quotations** where appropriate. Agree a **realistic timescale** for the work.

Specify the **copyright** situation. The starting point in law is that it belongs to the writer, but you may agree to allow ownership of it to the other person or that you will jointly own it. Provisions for what is to happen if you later get into disagreement can help, perhaps with a third party named or to be jointly agreed to be made **arbitrator**, if necessary.

I've just seen the jacket proposed by my publisher for my book and it's abysmal!

Oh, dear! Check your contract but it is unlikely that you will have any right to insist that the cover be changed. Publishers usually reserve the right to control production, along with advertising and distribution.

The best thing may be to **put your views** to the publisher as diplomatically as possible. If you can give good reasons for your reservations, the publisher may be open to alternatives or make modifications. However, it may then be suggested that you pay the **additional costs**. Perhaps you should take another look at the cover and see if it might grow on you. Publishers are usually the experts when it comes to what image will help a book sell.

10

Appreciating Legal Aspects of Self-Publishing

> I find more and more that my style of Designing is a Species by itself... resolv'd to shew an independence which I know will please an Author.
>
> (*Letter to the Reverend Dr Trusler*, William Blake)

IS IT FOR YOU?

If you are grappling with this question, you are in good company. Virginia Woolf, Beatrix Potter and John Galsworthy are just a few past pens who did so. More recently, Timothy Mo and Jill Paton Walsh once took this step then went on to be traditionally published. At the moment, Margaret James is proving another good example. There have also been instances of self-published books (formerly rejected) being picked up by top publishing houses such as Brian John's *Angel Mountain* novels. Some self-published works have gained great prestige, such as Preethi Nair's *Gypsy Masala,* or Mark Blayney's short story collection *Two Kinds of Silence* which won the Somerset Maughan Prize, or Julie Noble's *Talli's Secret*, which made the Whitbread longlist. Specialist non-fiction and children's books seem particularly suited to self-publishing. It has also become common with poetry, as very few major publishers take this, because it is usually less profitable.

For many fiction writers, self-publishing offers an alternative to unfavourable slush-pile odds and the stigma of vanity publishing. Non-fiction writers often feel they know their market better than any publisher. Costs have tumbled in recent years, with new digital printing technology.

Therefore assuming your answer is 'yes', several of the legal implications to bear in mind are discussed in this chapter.

CHOOSING THE TYPE OF ORGANISATION

As in any business venture, there is the issue of what form – or 'legal personality' – to take. Alternatives to operating as an individual include a **partnership**, a **limited company** or **an association such as a club**.

If you are effectively a 'one man band'/sole trader, you may be happy to carry on by yourself. You may still prefer to adopt a type of trade name. (When self-publishing a poetry collection with arts funding, I found it useful to have the name of *Nisaba Press* based on an ancient goddess of writing.) One very successful self-publisher, Vera Waters (www.verawaters.com) recommends adopting a name. It can add to your professional image and make negotiations with booksellers easier. There can sometimes be a tendency also for writers to under-sell themselves. Sometimes it helps to overcome this barrier, if you can see your 'product' under a third-party umbrella. If pooling resources with someone else, perhaps your spouse or a group of committed friends, you may become a partnership. The Partnership Act says this is:

> 'the relation which subsists between persons carrying on a business in common with a view of profit'.

You do not have to make a profit – only operate to achieve it. Nor do you need a written partnership agreement, although often (especially if partners are contributing money in unequal shares) it is a good idea to have one drawn up. Again, adopting a trade name may be appropriate.

FORMING A COMPANY

In deciding whether to become a company, you may need professional advice. One consideration is the limited liability which this brings. This means that, as a general rule, you cannot personally be sued for any debts (unlike in a partnership or as a sole trader). One group debated this choice but eventually opted to become a club to avoid expense and formality.

That said, these days you can get a company formed for you swiftly and for as little as around £50. Many organisations offer this service, including via the Internet (for example, AC Business Services Ltd at www.eacbs.com).

A club is usually a type of unincorporated association, which is a very loose form of entity and will normally not provide the limited liability of a company, with those involved often remaining individually liable for such as debts incurred by it. They can be simply an association of individuals who share a common purpose (such as the furtherance of writing), with a relatively informal constitution. At the other end of the spectrum, they can be an incorporated entity, normally registered as a 'company limited by guarantee', needing no share capital and limiting members' liability to a certain amount.

Companies have a constitution set out in a **Memorandum of Association**. This includes an objects clause (see below) and articles. Articles are rules to regulate the internal organisation, such as for meetings and company resolutions. A standard format called Table A may be adopted.

Objects clause

This states the objectives the company will have. It is important because technically the company can only act within such objectives. It is often lengthy, with subsections listing subsidiary aims and powers, such as the borrowing of money. Sometimes these include or are replaced by a simple statement that the company shall carry on business as a general commercial. There is usually a main objects clause, which encapsulates the primary aims.

A sample is set out in Figure 7. This involves a fictional company formed by two imaginary former partners, John Butler and Melanie Clark, who now require limited liability.

◆ Note that many company formalities are changing, with some being more simplified, with the full implementation of the Companies Act 2006 (currently due by October 2009).

Bearing in mind the tax position

Tax and National Insurance aspects are important because, depending upon your personal circumstances, one form may be more advantageous than another. You would ideally need to seek your accountant's advice over this.

As a business you will have to notify HMRC that you are trading.

CHOOSING A NAME

As previously indicated, you will probably adopt a business name to represent your imprint and give additional credibility. You may

Memorandum of Association of Butler and Clark Publishing Enterprises Limited

1. The name of the Company is Butler and Clark Publishing Enterprises Limited.

2. The registered office of the Company will be situated in England and Wales.

3. The objects for which the Company is established are:

   a. To carry on the business of self-publishers, including the publishing, selling, marketing and promotion of all types of books, magazines, leaflets and other literature, whether fiction or non-fiction.

   b. To carry on business as a general commercial company.

   c. To carry on any other business whatsoever which in the opinion of the Board of Directors is connected with or ancillary to the main business of the company as stated above.

Fig. 7. Sample extract of a Memorandum of Association, including the main objects clause.

find that your bank insists upon this when opening an account for your venture.

Avoid any name already in use or very similar to an existing name because of the risk of 'passing-off' (see Chapter 2) or anything misleading. Check for example with the Companies Registration Office (see addresses and websites at the back of this book) and in writers' handbooks. Also use a search engine to see what may be brought up to the Internet.

Your real name to appear on general stationery, receipts and invoices.

DEALING WITH OTHER FORMALITIES

International Standard Book Numbers/Barcodes

Published books need ISBNs and barcodes for proper listing. ISBNs are 13-digit reference numbers usually printed on a book's jacket and the verso (reverse/left-hand side) of any title page. They identify country of origin, publisher and the work concerned, and are allocated to books for sale by retail. ISBNs and barcodes enable it to be identified from where a book can be order.

You can obtain the numbers for books you intend to publish from the ISBN Agency (see addresses at the back of this book). They now usually have to be purchased in a block. Online service is via www.isbn.nielsonbookdata.co.uk. Your printers may offer a service to sort out these matters for you, depending on how much you want them to be involved and the fee you agree (see later).

An ISBN enables your book to be easily identified and traced by booksellers and potential readers. Chains such as W. H. Smith will not stock work without one. As some are now buying from self-publishers, why risk losing this chance for the sake of a technicality?

Book listing

The ISBN Agency can list your titles in certain useful directories. For example, Nik Morton of Morton Publishing, Gosport, self-published a niche crime novel and through listing received an order from London's Murder One crime bookshop.

Beware some of the mailshots you may receive as a result of listing, such as from printers and bookbinders. Money-saving offers on volume may leave you with too many books to sell.

British Library Cataloguing-in-Publication Data Programme

This is administered by the British Library with which a copy of the book is deposited (see addresses at the back of this book and www.bl.uk/aboutus/stratpolprog/legaldep/index.htm).

Depositing copies with Libraries

Under the Copyright Act of 1911 (since modified), publishers were placed under a duty to deposit a copy of any title, within one month of publication with the British Library and, if required, the following:

◆ The Bodleian Library, Oxford;

◆ The Library of Cambridge University;

♦ The Library of Trinity College, Dublin;

♦ The National Library of Scotland;

♦ The National Library of Wales.

You can send the British Library copy direct, and the others care of The Agency for the Legal Deposit Libraries (see addresses at the back of this book). These arrangements may change in the near future.

Advertising

A crucial aspect of self-publishing is marketing. Without a good strategy, your books may remain unsold. Selling through your own website can be very useful. (See later.)

Advertising methods include flyers, press releases, blurbs and hype of any description – but remember there are codes of advertising and sales promotion. The first principle of **The Advertising Code** is that:

'all advertisements should be legal, decent, honest and truthful.'

You can obtain advice on your advertising and promotions regarding the regulations from the Advertising Standards Authority (see addresses at the back of this book).

Title page

It is usual to include, on the verso (reverse) of this:

♦ the full name, address, telephone, email and website that you use as a publisher;

- the country where the book was printed;

- the name and address of the printer;

- a copyright notice (see Chapter 2) credits for such as anyone responsible for cover design or typesetting.

Assert your moral right

Don't forget that your right to be properly accredited as author must be asserted in writing (see Chapter 2). Usually you cover this in any publishing contract you enter. As self-publisher you are in control of this. Insert an assertion on the verso of the title page. (See example given in Chapter 2.)

Book-keeping and tax

Even if your self-publishing income is fairly low to start with, keep at least a cash book listing all your incomings and outgoings as they occur.

Provided you operate as a business to make a profit, you can normally claim any expenses against tax. Consult your accountant as necessary on the finer details.

A good accountant can often prove well worth the fees charged (which are usually tax deductible) and help minimise tax liability. Overall government information is also available at www.hmrc.gov.uk. The tax office provides free leaflets and a helpline.

Registering for VAT

You may find this unnecessary. The registration threshold from April 2008 is, in broad terms, set at an annual turnover of

£67,000. If you are likely to reach this or wish to apply for voluntary registration anyway, seek advice; for example, from your accountant.

If you are eligible to register, you may be able to reclaim any VAT charged (or inputted) to you; for example, VAT on printing costs.

TEAMING UP WITH A PRINTING FIRM

The range of services now on offer to self-publishers is very wide. There is much choice as regards the quality and depth of service you require and costs can be competitive. **Obtain quotes and make sure the expense is clearly itemised.**

The more help you need, the more this is likely to be reflected in the overall price. You may feel able to proceed with just straightforward conventional printing, rather than dealing with a firm that offers services and extras tailored to self-publishers.

Sourcing a printer

Recommendation from experienced self-publishers is probably the best way of sourcing a printer.

Many printers advertise in well-known writing magazines such as *Writers' News* or *Mslexia*. One of the more established firms with a good reputation is *Anthony Rowe*. Some may have particular experience in autobiography and the like, such as *Lifelines Press*. (See addresses and websites at the back of this book.)

Considerations to take into account

Many factors are involved on the printing side of self-publishing. Although not technically legal points, several of the major practical ones are set out below to assist you.

Litho or digital?

This is a basic choice about format that affects cost and is best discussed in detail with your printers.

Litho is generally used for longer runs (over 300) and offers a wider range of paper/binding possibilities. **Digital** used to be poorer quality overall but has improved in recent times. It is often cheaper for short runs and reprints, and offers a strong black image good for text but is more limited as regards the range of paper that can be used, with a relatively compressed tonal range. Both options now offer good quality for illustrations.

Print-run

To assist in deciding on this, do your market research to gauge likely sales. If in doubt, try a small digital print run as a pilot to see how sales go and to give as review copies. Then order your main print run based on anticipated sales from feedback received.

Paper

This can amount to 30–60% of total cost. Select the one best for your book, seeking the printers' advice.

Lamination

This can enhance the look of the book cover considerably but will add to cost.

Binding

This too has cost implications, so discuss this with your printers. Hardback is usually sewn, paperback unsewn.

Typography

Much of the early prejudice harboured by mainstream booksellers towards self-publishing arose because the quality of the typography was poor. It can now be excellent.

It may be best to stick to classic serif book typefaces such as Century or Palatino. Allow plenty of space for chapter headings, include decent margins and avoid having lines too close together, for reasons of easy readability.

Print on demand (POD)

See Chapter 7 for further background on this. Many printers and other outlets now offer print on demand. Advantages include **minimal stockholding, eliminating storage costs, and smaller initial investment**.

Amazon has recently launched a POD service to rival such as Lulu.com, Lightning Source UK and Blurb.com. Interestingly, in connection with its new Kindle reader device (see Chapter 6), Amazon has also launched its 'Digital Text Platform', which could allow writers to upload manuscripts to its Kindle Store and have them converted into *Kindle* books.

Terms to bear in mind with printers

Whatever you decide, **make sure any agreement is recorded in writing and check any contract and/or standard terms you are asked to sign are reasonable and accord with what you have in mind.** Bear in mind also the general contract points covered in Chapter 5.

In reaching any agreement with a printing firm, ensure that:

◆ all copyright and subsidiary rights remain with you and you grant no rights to the printers;

- the total amount to be paid by you is spelt out and itemised clearly, including any extras such as obtaining ISBN;

- your production requirements, such as print-run, are made clear;

- it is decided where the books are to be stored, for example, whether delivered to your home for this or stored by the printers, and that there is appropriate insurance cover;

- it is noted under what circumstances you could terminate the agreement (for example, undue delay by the printers) and obtain a refund or appropriate partial refund of any money paid.

Getting other help

You may need to seek help from other specialists as well as your printers. This will depend on what services they can offer and your own level of expertise.

You might, for example, need to consult a **freelance editor**, a **proofreader**, a **typesetter and/or a graphic designer**. The design of your cover will prove especially important to saleability. (Sometimes graphic design or art college students are willing to help at very reasonable rates.)

You may also consider finding a **distributor**. Your printers may help with this or the Independent Publishers Guild may be able to assist (see addresses at the back of this book). You may also be able to join such as Amazon's current 'Advantage Programme', though certain criteria apply.

Make sure any terms agreed are confirmed in writing and are in line with your intentions. Bear in mind also the general contract points referred to in Chapter 5 and the points above regarding terms agreed with printers.

Permissions
Do not forget that you will need copyright clearance for any quotations or illustrations that you intend to use in your work (see Chapter 3).

PROMOTING YOUR WORK
Whilst promotion can involve fewer legal aspects than other parts of the self-publishing process, it is vital to success. Basic points involved are outlined here and the tips included are collected from several experienced self-publishers.

You may have begun to think of yourself as a publisher as well as a writer, but it also helps to add **publicist** and **entrepreneur** to your roles. You should try to publicise your work by as many ways as is appropriate. Use any contacts you have and draw up your own marketing plan. This could include the following areas set out below.

Contacting booksellers
Persuading booksellers to stock your title, even on a **sale or return** basis, may prove one of the most challenging parts of self-publishing. (A thick skin can help.) There is no magic formula for success but make contact with all those you can and stress your book's **selling points**. You may find you have to **negotiate discounts**.

Judging a book by its cover
An eye-catching book cover is a major marketing device. The **design** is important. Interesting **blurb** on the back about you and your work can help, perhaps also with a photograph. If possible,

obtain and include comments/'sound-bites' on your work from relevant well-known people or authors.

Attracting publicity

Draft a **press release** to send to newspapers. Local ones in particular like to feature writers from their area. They may ask you for an interview and arrange for a photograph to be taken.

Local radio also likes to interview writers. Often these sessions may be as much about you and your life as about your book.

If your book ties in with any **topical event** or **historical anniversary**, emphasise this in order to generate interest. Also consider attending the **London Book Fair**, usually held in April each year (www.londonbookfair.co.uk).

Should you hold a launch party?

A launch party, perhaps at your home rather than incurring room hire charges, can help kick-start sales. Sending out invitations can be a useful way to make contact with those who could be interested in your book, even if they prove unable to attend.

Giving talks and readings

These can be an excellent way of publicising your work and selling books.

One successful self-publisher, Les Baynton, has produced several children's poetry collections and spends much time working in schools and giving readings (www.pintpotpoetry.co.uk). This has also led to travelling far afield and interesting spin-offs such as giving workshops on Roald Dahl at a theatre.

You may not always be able to **negotiate a fee**, especially for bookshop readings. If you can, **reasonable rates** currently vary but can be around £250 per day plus expenses. A decent fee is more likely to be paid where you are an expert in your field and/or a sizeable audience will be drawn to see you. **Arts festivals** can give good author appearance opportunities.

Bear in mind that for schools and similar organisations, **certain preliminary checks** may have to be carried out on you first and you may need to have some form of **public liability insurance**. Make sure that you are fully aware of and observe any conditions of this insurance (for example there may be a requirement to have a teacher in attendance) to ensure that it is not invalidated.

Conferences and groups relevant to the subject area of your work may also be a likely source of your becoming a guest speaker. Also consider giving **talks to writers' groups and at libraries**.

USING THE INTERNET

Do you need a website?

This has to be of advantage to any self-publisher. You can use your website to publicise yourself and your work, and to **sell books through it**. Some self-publishers have done this with great success. John P Strecky has been reported as selling some 10,000 copies of his *The why are you here café* through his website alone.

You can give a link to Amazon, if your book is also available there. If you sell direct from your website, you may need to offer **credit card facilities** through a service like **Paypal**.

What about a blog?

A recent survey suggests that around four million belong to Britain's growing community of bloggers. Blogs began a few years ago mainly as **online diaries** but have now developed beyond this. You can still use them as diaries, but they can also carry **news of a writer's activities** or be used as an addition to a website for material that does not fit well there. Information on setting up a blog is available from such as www.blogginghelp.com and www.squidoo.com/blogstarter/.

Described as 'the new blogging' by some, **wikis** are online communities that can be useful to writers. Try, for example, digital news at http://digitalnews.wikispaces.com for news and tips on online journalism.

Link your blog to your website, if you have both.

CASE STUDIES

Liz gets an offer

Liz is dismayed at the trouble in placing her latest novel, which she has completed after a year's hard work. It is more experimental than her previous work.

She is cheered by a win in a national short story competition. As a result, she gives an interview on local radio, discussing her work in general. She later receives a letter purporting to offer to publish her novel. After the rejections she has received, she is tempted by 'the chance to see your work in print at a fair price' stated in the letter.

Liz has almost certainly been mailshotted by a subsidy publisher, who perhaps obtained her name and address after hearing the interview. She would be well-advised to look beyond any enticing statements in initial correspondence.

The Advertising Standards Authority previously researched into advertising practices of the 'vanity press'. The main concern was that advertisers might mislead clients on promotion intended for each book and the potential profits. The Committee of Advertising Practice issued an *Advice Note* directed at such publishers.

That is not to say that there are not some reputable subsidy publishers who can offer a worthwhile service.

It is doubtful, however, whether this is something for Liz. She could persevere with trying to find another publisher. Alternatively she could opt for self-publishing; for example, using desk-top facilities. These have become much cheaper in recent times, though prices of systems fluctuate and dealers will negotiate. It may represent a better investment for her than contributing to subsidy publishing, and this way she will be in control.

Bill the poet

Several of Bill's poems have been accepted in fairly respectable small press literary publications, but he cannot find any publisher who will bring out a volume.

The market for poetry is limited. This has made some poets particularly susceptible to misleading claims of less scrupulous vanity publishers, as highlighted some years ago by Johnathon Clifford of the former National Poetry Foundation.

Bill may find self-publishing is a suitable option. Poetry is difficult to sell, but he may have a sufficiently wide circle of friends or contacts who will be interested. He may intend local distribution only. Organised readings may help. He will probably not wish to invest in desk-top equipment. He could consider contracting-out the printing. Most reputable printers will do short runs or he could approach a self-publishing agency. He could also set his material on disc, passing it on to a specialist firm to typeset and continue to full book finishing. Technical services of this nature can be found through the trade press or writers magazines. Bill should obtain written quotes and stipulate a deadline for completion of the work. He could also try the Arts Council, regarding grant assistance possibilities (though much arts funding has been cut back recently).

Daniel and the anthology

Daniel belongs to a playwrights' group. With so few plays published, members decide to collaborate on producing an anthology of their works.

One of the main decisions to be taken is the amount each will contribute to the venture. They need to produce an estimate of the expense to ascertain this. If they intend to sell the anthology at a profit, they may decide to operate as a partnership (usual maximum, twenty). It would be advisable to have a written agreement to record the respective contributions and other terms agreed. In particular, provision should be included for how the partnership can be dissolved (brought to an end). (See also Chapter 9 on collaboration aspects.)

SUMMARY

- ◆ Decide if self-publishing is a good move for your particular writing career.

- ◆ If so, there are technicalities to note – but not to deter you.

- ◆ Decide on how you will operate and the form of business you wish to take. Take professional advice as necessary.

- ◆ In choosing a name ensure this is not too similar to an existing name and is not misleading.

- ◆ Bear in mind formalities, such as ISBN, book listing, library copies, advertising regulations and assertion of your moral rights.

- ◆ Consult your accountant as necessary regarding book-keeping and tax, particularly VAT if applicable.

POINTS TO CONSIDER

1. Consider which form of business venture you would be most likely to take as a self-publisher.

2. A self-publisher must be 'hands on' as regards book production. List the types of formalities you would have to bear in mind as a self-publisher, which would not concern you as simply an author.

3. Which kind of titles do you feel would be especially suited to self-publishing?

11

Dealing With Your Literary Estate

So long as men can breathe or eyes can see
So long lives this and this gives life to thee.

Sonnet XVIII, Shakespeare)

MAKING A WILL

In making a will, it is advisable to consult a professional. Lawyers often remark that they make more money out of 'home-made' wills than those they draft themselves, due to disputes which can later arise over defects. Many solicitors charge a relatively modest fee (often in the hope that if the will remains lodged with them, they will have a chance of later getting the job of administering the estate).

All authors should take into account their literary estate when making a will. If published, you may require a particular person to inherit royalties. Even if unpublished, you may wish to leave your work in the hands of someone likely to safeguard it.

You can bequeath (give in your will) an original manuscript. It is implied with an unpublished manuscript that copyright of the work passes with it. Alternatively, you can specify in your will to whom copyright/the right to receive royalties is to go. Your moral rights (see Chapter 2) usually pass to the person inheriting the copyright but you can nominate someone else to take these over. The paternity and integrity rights last as long as the copyright. The right against false attribution expires 20 years after your death and is only actionable by your personal representatives (usually the executors named in your will). Public Lending Right (see Chapter 6) is normally bequeathed with copyright.

CHOOSING THE RIGHT EXECUTORS

Executors carry out the will. The beneficiaries inherit under it. They can be one and the same, or different people.

Executors and beneficiaries named in respect of your general property may not be your preference to entrust with your writings. If you name no executors, or die intestate (without a will), your next of kin under the intestacy rules take over. You may prefer to make express provision.

If you have an agent, he/she may be the obvious choice to take over your literary estate. The term 'literary executor' is not a legal one but will probably be used by the agent. You may appoint the agent to be in effect a trustee of your literary assets for the benefit of named beneficiaries. Alternatively, you could just request that the 'literary executor' advise the main executors regarding your literary assets.

If you are unpublished, you may prefer writer-friends to take charge of your works, or persons to whom you feel they were indirectly dedicated. Your autobiography may, for example, be important to your grandchildren.

PLANNING FOR THE FUTURE

Legal problems can arise in leaving money to promote your work after your death. The law will not usually allow a trust set up indefinitely for a purpose, rather than to benefit a group or an individual. Exceptions exist, such as for charities (which are now subject to more stringent criteria under the Charities Act 2006), and there are ways round the matter. One alternative is to leave money to a friend and express a hope that they will use it for the purpose you require. This area is, however, in general hedged with many technical rules, making specialist legal drafting advisable.

You could leave the right to royalties or a lump sum to a relevant charity; for example, the Royal Literary Fund.

TAKING TAX INTO ACCOUNT

The Revenue are not usually unreasonable when it comes to agreeing probate valuations of literary estates. Estimates by your publisher or agent will be relevant. Inheritance tax must be borne in mind when your will is drafted. You may need professional advice on minimising tax, perhaps by lifetime transfers or appropriate provision in your will (though the higher thresholds introduced in 2007 make this less common a problem).

CASE STUDIES

Each of the three writers you have followed through the case studies would consider their position regarding their respective literary estates according to their own particular circumstances. A brief overview of the possibilities is considered below.

Liz

Liz's executor for her general estate will probably be her husband. She may be happy for him also to administer her literary matters – particularly if he is the sole beneficiary under her will, and is therefore to receive royalties from her work.

Bill

Bill may wish to nominate a writer-friend to take control of his literary estate, or perhaps a relative who has encouraged him in his writing.

Daniel

Daniel would doubtless appoint his agent as 'literary executor'. He should ensure that the agent is given full control in copyright matters, so that any infringement can be properly challenged and Daniel's work fully safeguarded.

SUMMARY

♦ It is advisable to have your will professionally drawn up.

♦ Give careful consideration to whom you name as suitable to take over your literary estate.

♦ Specialist drafting may be required if you wish to give directions on the future promotion of your work.

POINTS TO CONSIDER

1. Why do you think it is important that an author's work is left in safe hands?

2. Consider why it may be advisable to appoint a specific 'literary executor'.

3. What do you feel are the characteristics which a good 'literary executor' should have?

Glossary

ALCS. Authors Licensing and Collecting Society.

Acknowledgement. Written credit to the author of a source used.

Case law. Body of legal precedents, comprising decisions in previous cases.

CD-Rom (Compact Disk Read-Only Memory). A compact disk with fixed data, such as text, graphics, audio, video clips and animation with 3-D potential.

Contract. A legally binding agreement.

Damages. Money compensation awarded by civil courts.

Defamation. A **tort** concerning injury to reputation through such things as untrue statements.

Digitisation. The conversion of material into electronic form.

Directives. A form of European legislation.

Domain name. A type of user's registered 'address' on the Internet, from which his/her website is generally derived.

EEA. European Economic Area.

e-book. Text produced in PDF and made available to read via electronic or similar forms of transmission.

E-mail (electronic mail). A means of electronic communication, usually via the Internet.

Encryption. Technical methods (often using cyphers, codes and cryptography) which may help prevent access to the copying of electronic material.

Equity. A body of English law based upon equitable principles of fairness.

Estoppel. A legal doctrine which can sometimes prevent someone denying a previous statement or going back on a promise.

Fair dealing. An exception to usual copyright restrictions.

Injunction. A court order to prevent, or sometimes compel, certain action.

Intellectual property. Creative material which can be protected by copyright, trademarks, patents and/or design law.

Internet (the Net). A global network, linking computers.

Law. References in this book are generally to the law of England and Wales, and as it applies mainly to British persons.

Legislation. Laws embodied in forms such as Acts of Parliament or statutory instruments.

Libel. **Defamation** in a permanent form.

Licence. A permission, usually in writing, for a certain act.

Litigation. Disputes involving court proceedings.

MTA – Minimum Terms Agreement.

Magistrates. Justices of the Peace, who are usually lay persons, not legally qualified, who hear criminal cases in the magistrates' courts.

Mediation. A method of trying to reconcile a dispute, usually through someone who acts as a type of go-between.

Moral rights. Legal rights associated with copyright and aimed at protecting reputation.

Multimedia. Presentation of material (often digital), using more than two media (often interactive).

NUJ. National Union of Journalists.

Online. Connected to systems in communication with a computer, often via a telephone network.

PDF. Portable document format.

POD. Print on demand.

Passing-off. A **tort** concerning a claim that someone has wrongly represented goods or work as being associated with someone else.

Patent. Legal means of protecting an invention from use by another.

Plagiarism. A pejorative term for using someone else's work.

Public domain. When a work is no longer protected by copyright, it is said to have entered this.

RRP. Recommended retail price.

Slander. In broad terms, **defamation** in a non-permanent, usually verbal form.

Tort. A civil wrong for which an individual can sue in the civil courts.

Trademark. An identification symbol, slogan or other device or sign (usually used in marketing) which can be registered as a trademark.

Trading Standards Departments. Local departments which enforce legislation such as The Trade Descriptions Act and which can help consumers against unscrupulous commercial practices.

Trust. The legal means by which property or money is held by a trustee for the benefit of another (the beneficiary).

Typographical arrangement. The arrangement of printed words.

Will. A document which seeks to enforce the wishes of a person after their death in relation to their property.

Useful Addresses and Websites

The Advertising Standards Authority, Mid City Place, 71 High Holborn, London WC1V 6QT. Tel: (020) 7492 2222.

Anthony Rowe, Bumper's Farm, Chippenham, Wiltshire SN14. 6LH. Tel: (01249) 659705.

The Agency for the Legal Deposit Libraries, 100 Euston Street, London NW1 2HQ. Tel: (020) 7388 5061.

The Association of Authors' Agents, c/o Penny Holroyde, Caroline Sheldon Literary Agency Ltd, 70–75 Courcross Street, London EC1M 6EJ. Tel: (020) 7336 8550.

The Authors' Licensing and Collecting Society (ALCS), The Writers' House, 13 Haydon Street, London EC3N 1DB. Tel: (020) 7264 5700.

British Association of Lawyer Mediators, The Shooting Lodge, Guildford Road, Sutton Green, Guildford GU4 7PZ. Tel: 07000 766422.

The British Copyright Council, Copyright House, 29–33 Berner Street, London W1T 3AB. Tel: (01986) 788122.

The British Library, Legal Deposit Office, Boston Spa, Wetherby LS23 7BQ. Tel: 0870 441500.

Companies House, Crown Way, Cardiff CF14 3UZ. Tel: 0870 3333636.

The Copyright Licensing Agency Ltd, Saffron House, 6–10 Kirby Street, London EC1N 8TS. Tel: (020) 7400 3100.

The Independent Publishers Guild, PO Box 93, Royston, Hertfordshire SG8 5GH.

The Information Commissioner's Offices, Wycliffe House, Water Lane, Wilmslow, Cheshire SK9 5AF. Tel: 08456 306060.

The Intellectual Property Office, Central Enquiry Unit, Cardiff Road, Newport, South Wales NP10 8QQ. Tel: 08459 500505.

The ISBN Agency/Neilsen Registration Services, c/o EDItEUR, 39–41 North Road, London N7 9DA. Tel: (020) 7607 0021.

Lifelines Press, 58 Queens Road, Tunbridge Wells, Kent TN4 9JU. Tel: (01892) 512323.

The National Union of Journalists, Headland House, 312 Gray's Inn Road, London WC1X 8DP. Tel: (020) 7278 7916.

The Newspaper Licensing Agency Ltd, Wellington Gate, Church Road, Tunbridge Wells, Kent TN1 1NL. Tel: (01892) 525273.

The Press Complaints Commission, HaltonHouse, 20–23 Holborn, London EC1N 2SD. Tel: (020) 7831 0022.

The Public Lending Right Office, Richard House, Sorbonne Close, Stockton-on-Tees, Cleveland TS17 6DA. Tel: (01642) 604699.

The Publishers Association, 29 Montague Street, London WC1B 5BW. Tel: (020) 7691 9191.

The Royal Literary Fund, 3 Johnson's Court, London EC4A 3EA. Tel: (020) 7353 7159.

The Society of Authors, 84 Drayton Gardens, London SW10 9SB. Tel: (020) 7373 6642.

The Society of Women Writers and Journalists (membership), c/o 27 Braycourt Avenue, Walton-on-Thames KT12 2AZ.

VAT Central Unit, Alexander House, 21 Victoria Avenue, Southend-on-Sea SS99 1AA. Tel: 08450 109000.

The Writers' Guild of Great Britain, 15 Britannia Street, London WC1X 9JN. Tel: (020) 7833 0777.

Websites

www.agentsassoc.co.uk

www.alcs.co.uk

www.allpartywritersgroup.co.uk

www.amazon.co.uk

www.anthonyrowe.co.uk

www.artscouncil.org.uk

www.artscape.co.uk

www.arvonfoundation.org

www.asa.org.uk

www.askaboutwriting.net

www.authorsregister.com

www.bbc.co.uk/writersroom

www.bl.uk

www.blogger.com

www.booktrust.org.uk

www.britishcopyright.org

www.britishprint.com

www.cafepress.com

www.ccskills.org.uk

www.cedr.co.uk

www.cla.co.uk

www.companies-house.gov.uk

www.contactanauthor.co.uk

www.createspace.com

www.creativecommons.org

www.eacbs.com

www.euroscript.co.uk

www.expertsources.co.uk

www.familyrecords.gov.uk

www.foi.gov.uk

www.freelancersintheuk.co.uk

www.googledebate.com

www.howtobooks.co.uk

www.hmcourts-service.gov.uk

www.hmrc.gov.uk

www.ico.gov.uk

www.ilkleyliteraturefestival.org.uk

www.informationcommissioner.gov.uk

www.indexers.org.uk

www.intellectual-property.gov.uk

www.ipo.gov.uk

www.ipg.uk.com

www.isbn.nielsenbook.co.uk

www.lifelinespress.com

www.literaturetraining.com

www.londonbookfair.co.uk

www.londonfreelance.org

www.lulu.com

www.meettheauthor.co.uk

www.moneyclaim.gov.uk

www.mslexia.co.uk

www.ncll.org.uk

www.newplaysnw.com

www.nibweb.co.uk

www.nielsonbookdata.co.uk

www.nla.co.uk

www.nuj.org.uk

www.patent.gov.uk

www.pcc.org.uk

www.pintpotpoetry.co.uk

www.plagiarism.org

www.own-it.org

www.readingagency.org.uk

www.rlf.org.uk

www.rslit.org.uk

www.scenaristes.org

www.screenwritersfestival.com

www.scriptfactory.co.uk

www.scriptyorkshire.co.uk

www.societyofauthors.org

www.swwj.co.uk

www.traceline.co.uk

www.transita.co.uk

www.watch-file.com

www.writersbookshelf.co.uk

www.writersguild.org.uk

www.writersandartists.co.uk

www.writernet.org.uk

www.wss.org.uk

Note The author/publisher have made reasonable efforts to ensure that the addresses and URLs for websites are correct and active at the time of writing, but no guarantee can be given that these will remain current/live or that content will remain appropriate.

Further Reading

From Pitch to Publication, Carole Blake (Macmillan, 1999)

An Author's Guide to Publishing, Michael Legat (Robert Hale, 1998)

A User's Guide to Copyright, M. Flint, N. Fitzpatrick and C. Thorne, 6th edition (Tottel Publishing, 2006)

McNae's Essential Law for Journalists, Tom Welsh, Walter Grenwood and David Banks, 19th edition (Oxford, 2007)

Copyright Made Easier, Raymond A Wall, (Europa Publications, 2000 ISBN 0851424473)

Writers' Guide to Getting Published, Chriss McCallum (How To Books, 2003 ISBN 1 85703 8770)

Publishing Law, Hugh Jones (Routledge, 2000 ISBN 0415 15466 9)

The Cassell Handbook of Copyright in British Publishing Practice, J. M. Cavendish and K. Pool, 3rd edition (1993, ISBN 0 30432635 6)

The Writers' and Artists' Yearbook (A & C Black, 2008 ISBN 9-7807 13683714)

The Poetry Writers' Yearbook (A & C Black, 2008)

The Screenwriter's Handbook (Macmillan, 2008)

The Internet: A Writer's Guide, Jane Dorner (A & C Black, 2000 ISBN 071 36612 67)

Intellectual Property, David Bainbridge, 7th edition (Pearson Education, 2008)

Research for Writers, Anne Hoffman (A & C Black, 2008)

How to Publish Your Own Book, Anna Crosbie (How To Books, 2006)

Marketing Your Book: An Author's Guide, Alison Baverstock, 2nd
edition (A & C Black 2008 ISBN 9-780713-673838)
*The Easy Step by Step Guide to Publishing and Promoting Your
Book*, Pauline Rowson (Rowmark, 2006)
Writing for Pleasure and Profit, Michael Legat (Robert Hale,
2008)

Useful magazines

Mslexia, PO Box 656 Freepost NEA S66. Newcastle-Upon-Tyne
NE1 1BR. www.mslexia.co.uk
Writers' News, Warner Group Publications plc, 31–32 Park Row,
Leeds LS1 5JD. www.writersnews.co.uk
Writing Magazine (address as for *Writers' News*)
www.writingmagazine.co.uk
The Author, published by the Society of Authors (see Useful
Addresses)

Index

The Creative Writer's Workbook
Cathy Birch

'...exudes confidence and optimism...full of devices to make the imagination flow.' – Alison Chisholm, BBC Radio Merseyside

'Your true writer's voice is unlikely to inhabit the realms of logic...this book takes you on a journey into the subconscious to help you find that voice – and use it. The results can be both amazing and satisfying.' – *Writer's Own*

'There is a solid, practical base to this book...Give Cathy's methods a try, you might surprise yourself.' – *Writers' Bulletin*

ISBN 978-1-84528-306-3

The Beginner's Guide to Getting Published
Chriss McCallum

'Absorbing and highly informative...No author seriously interested in getting published can afford to be without this book.' – *Writers' News*

'Really definitive...Leaves every other similar book in its shade.' – *Pause, National Poetry Foundation*

'Worth every penny. If you're really serious about being published, this book should be your bible.' – *Writers' Bulletin*

'...should be on any beginner's reading list.' – *Writers Forum*

ISBN 978-1-85703-217-2

The Beginners' Guide to Writing a Novel
Marina Oliver

'An excellent introduction for the new novelist.' – *Writing Magazine*

'What I like about Marina's approach is the emphasis she places on characterisation...she shows how to make characters compelling, how to keep the pages turning. There isn't one piece of advice, one tip or suggestion for further reading that isn't full of practical common-sense.' – *Writers' Bulletin*

ISBN 978-1-84528-091-8

The Five-Minute Writer
Margret Geraghty

'I purchased this book on a whim, hoping to obtain some creative genius to help me write. I was pleasantly surprised by how much it helped me in my time of great need to achieve ideas and comfort me in my period of writer's block. Outstanding work by Geraghty...I attribute (hopefully) my success in the future. A must for first-time writers!' – Reader review

'An exploration of ritualistic behaviour, thinking outside the box, writing about the concept of choice. Just three of the 57 topics and they are presented in a way that stimulates your creative thinking process.' – *Writing Magazine*

This book will inspire you to write – even if you have only a few minutes a day to spare. Each chapter offers you a writing-related discussion, followed by a five-minute exercise. Just pick a page and begin your writer's journey.

ISBN 978-1-84528-339-1

How To Write Short Stories For Magazines
Sophie King

'An Invaluable source of tips and inside information from writers and magazines editors.' – *Good Book Guide*

Writing short stories is both a science and an art. You need a certain amount of skill but you will increase your chances by studying your market and learning what magazine editors are looking for. It is not always obvious. This book will take you as a would-be writer through the tricks of the trade by helping you discover what the different magazines are looking for and how to think up ideas to suit; demonstrating how you can write different slants, such as twist in the tales and feel-good stories; advising on how you can win fiction competitions.

ISBN 978-1-84528-280-6

Writing from Life
Lynne Hackles

'I suggest you take it with you when you travel to work . . . You will begin thinking and often those times are the moments to begin a new journey. The book will prod you onward. Highly recommended.' – *www.london-morning-paper.co.uk*

'Her excellent book demonstrates that writing about what you know really is the way into print, whether you are writing non-fiction or fiction.' – *Writing Magazine*

'Practical techniques that will make it easier.' – *Good Book Guide*

ISBN 978-1-84528-241-7

How To Set Up a Freelance Writing Business
Jason Deign

Get paid for what you like doing best – make a living from your writing.

'Here is all the advice you need on setting up and running your freelance business, with lots of tips on kitting yourself out, on book-keeping and so forth. This book is also strong on copywriting skills.' – *Writers' News*

ISBN 978-1-84528-257-8

Creative Writing
Adèle Ramet

'This is a book which merits a place on every writer's bookshelf.' – *Writers' Bulletin*

'...an excellent book for the beginner writer. Packed with examples and case studies, this is not a book that just deals in theory.' – *Writers' News*

ISBN 978-1-84528-101-4

How To Write a Thriller
Scott Mariani

'I just wish this book had been around when I was starting out. It's highly engaging, inspirational and full of useful insights...just like a great thriller itself, I couldn't put it down! Reading this book should be the first step for any budding thriller writer.' Seth Garner, author of *The Blood Partnership* and *Broken Surface*
'highly engaging, inspirational and full of useful insights...' – Seth Garner

ISBN 978-1-84528-163-2

How To Books are available through all good bookshops, or you can order direct from us through Grantham Book Services.

Tel: +44 (0)1476 541080
Fax: +44 (0)1476 541061
Email: orders@gbs.tbs-ltd.co.uk

Or via our website

www.howtobooks.co.uk

To order via any of these methods please quote the title(s) of the book(s) and your credit card number together with its expiry date.

For further information about our books and catalogue, please contact:

How To Books
Spring Hill House
Spring Hill Road
Begbroke
Oxford
OX5 1RX

Visit our web site at
www.howtobooks.co.uk

Or you can contact us by email at info@howtobooks.co.uk